Kisses from SARDINIA

A REMARKABLE MEMOIR

LAURIE PILIA

The library of congress has catalogued the paperback edition as follows: Kisses from Sardinia: A Remarkable Memoir / by Laurie Pilia
ISBN: 978-1-7343208-2-4

1. Inspiration 2. Relationships 3. Adventure 4. Romance 5.Women

*Some names and identifying details have been changed to protect the privacy of individuals.

This book is dedicated to my beautiful Carlo, Sofia, and Nora! You make my life complete.

Table of Contents

"You Want Hash Browns
with that Baby?"

I opened my eyes to a strange feeling. Slowly, I rolled out of bed—literally *rolled*—as I had been doing for the last three months or so. I struggled to my feet and looked over at my husband, John, who was still sound asleep. He was pressed up against the wall on the far side of the mattress—a necessary evil since I had to get up and go to the bathroom so often in the night. I looked at the strip of early summer sunshine between the curtains, wondering what time it was. Then, I felt it: the warm gush of water between my legs and the *pit-pat-pit-pat* sound as it dribbled onto the beige carpet. At first, I thought I had lost control of myself, but a moment later I realized that today was the day.

"John! Wake up!" I yelled as I ran for the bathroom.

I sat down on the toilet, listening for any sound from the bedroom... *nothing.*

"John! It's time to wake up!"

When I felt like it was safe to get up from the toilet, I went back into the bedroom. John's head was buried in the pillow and he was snoring. I shook him until his eyes finally peeled open. His pupils darted back and forth as if he had no idea where he was.

"I think my water broke!" I said. "You need to get up. We need to leave now."

I went back to the bathroom, brushed my teeth and then began to gather the things I would need at the hospital. John continued to lie in bed. I was incredulous as I jerked a T-shirt over my head. *How can he just lie there?* To be honest, John's self-absorption was not a huge shock to me. I had endured it throughout our relationship. Like any young, naive woman, however, I thought he might grow up at some point, that he would "change". Naturally, I was hurt by his response at such a life-altering moment. He wasn't anxious to see his own child? But, I didn't have time to deal with his immaturity.

"John! Please get up! We need to get to the hospital!"

He stretched and groaned. "I need to take a shower first," he said.

"What do you mean *shower*? There's no time! You can shower later. Let's go!"

He reluctantly got up and grabbed his jeans off the floor. I went out and put our things in the back seat of my white '96 Toyota Camry. John emerged from the house, yawning.

"I'm too tired to drive," he moaned.

I stood in the driveway, staring at him. I thought I would scream. "Fine!" I said, jumping into the driver's seat. Moments later, we turned out of our neighborhood onto the main highway. It was a bright and warm late- May morning.

"Take the next exit," John said.

I had a death grip on the steering wheel as I looked over at him. "Why?" I asked.

"I want to hit the Burger King drive-through. I'm hungry."

It was all I could do not to cry. I wasn't having any contractions yet, but I was desperate to get to the hospital. I was twenty-five years old, it was my first baby, and I was scared. I let out a ragged sigh and pulled off at the exit. Though it was probably less than five minutes, it was the longest time I'd ever spent in a drive-through while John ordered his ham, egg, and cheese croissant.

At last, we arrived at the hospital. A young blonde triage nurse took us into a small examination room.

"Are you having any pain?" she asked.

"No," I told her. "But I think my water broke. I am four days past my due date."

The nurse examined me and confirmed that my water had broken, but that I wasn't dilated and would have to be induced. I had read about such things, but really had no idea what the next several hours would bring—except for a baby, of course. John and I were ushered to a spacious delivery room with a couch, TV, several chairs and a lot of medical equipment.

I met Sandy, my labor and delivery nurse, and was soon put on an IV drip of Pitocin. I settled in on the bed and grabbed the TV remote as John relaxed in a lounge chair. As I watched *Dr. Phil,* the small, sharp contractions began. My body was beginning to do its work. Soon, I would see my child. I was excited and scared all at the same time. John acted as if he were waiting to get his oil changed, sitting back and staring at the TV, saying nothing. I looked over at him occasionally, hoping he would take an interest in what was happening. I should have known better: he wasn't the center of attention.

At last, my parents arrived. I instantly felt better. Their faces were glowing with excitement to meet their first grandchild. Minutes later, my Aunt Lynn, Mom's younger sister, arrived. Aunt Lynn, a gregarious brunette who contrasted to my mother's more reserved personality, was a close confidant, someone with whom I shared things that were too intense to tell my parents. They all embraced me, asking me how I was feeling.

"I'm going to run home and take a shower," John announced suddenly.

My father's expression darkened. I had seen that look before: he was about to give my husband a piece of his mind. "You need to stay here, son. Your wife is in labor."

I think John got the hint that this was not a suggestion, but an order. He screwed up his face and fell back into the lounge chair.

My best friends Pamela and Abigail walked in about that time. Abigail had brought her camera, ready to photograph the blessed event. As my contractions intensified, I began to shift and squirm.

"Breathe, Laurie," my mother said. "You have to breathe."

After a couple of hours, my obstetrician Dr. Lin, a Chinese woman who reminded me of "Dora the Explorer", arrived. I was relieved to see her and not one of the other doctors who shared her rotation. After checking me, she ordered an epidural. I had a white-knuckle grip on the bed rails: *About time…*

After the epidural was administered, John's mother, Jenny walked in. She, like my parents, was eager to see her grandchild.

When my pain went from a 9 to a 2, I was ready for a nap. I slept while my family, friends, and various medical personnel wandered in and out. I awoke a short time later and chatted with everyone. At around 4:15 pm, Dr. Lin returned. She checked my cervix.

"It's time to have a baby," she said. "Anyone who wants to stay, can."

My dad opted out while everyone else stayed. Even John was suddenly interested: he was fumbling with the camcorder and tripod at the foot of the bed. I just wanted to hold my baby. Abigail served as coach, propping me up as Dr. Lin told me to push. Mom and Aunt Lynn each had a leg, giving me words of encouragement as they followed the doctor's lead. Things seemed to take forever. I was exhausted from pushing.

"I can see the head!" Dr. Lin said. *At last.*

At 5:23 pm, with one final, agonizing push—my mother and Lynn weeping in awe—my precious Sofia Marie came into the world.…

Small Town Girls

When I was born in April of 1980, my mother's childbirth experience was far different from mine. My mother was a sophomore in high school when she discovered she was pregnant at the age of fifteen. My grandparents were divorced, and my mother lived with her mother, Nancy, and her two younger siblings, Lynn and Bob, in the town of Milford Center, Ohio.

Susan Evans was like many other teenagers. She was a cheerleader who excelled at school, liked boys and hanging out with her friends. Her mom, my grandma, had moved around a lot, so friendships could be fleeting. She managed to maintain one enduring friendship with a girl named Deena.

One night during the summer between my mother's freshman and sophomore year, she and Deena met up with some older guys for a night of fun. The events of that evening would change my mother's life forever.

My Aunt Lynn, who was fourteen at the time, remembers listening through the door of my mother's bedroom in their old brick farmhouse in the country as my mother sobbed and told my grandmother about her suspicions. When the conversation became clear to her, she burst through the door and shouted, "Are we having a baby?" My aunt, in her words, was "over the moon".

My mother, however, was young and scared. She had options, of course, but in the end, she chose to have me. My grandmother decided to move the family to Marysville, Ohio shortly after. My mother elected to have a tutor come to her home during her sophomore year, not wanting to attend a new school as a pregnant teen. My mom also babysat for two young girls while their mother worked second shift. It wasn't long before the family moved again. This time, they moved in with my grandmother's boyfriend, Roger, who, according to my mother's recollections, had a beard and long hair and looked like a "mountain man or a hippie". He also grew his own marijuana. My mother didn't like living with Roger at the time, but in later years she recalled he was a kind and gentle man who was very generous to open his home to her mother and her three children.

One warm spring day in April, my grandmother drove my mother to her thirty-eight-week OB/GYN appointment. The doctor said it would likely be another week and that things looked good. On the way home, they stopped at the local mall and then at a friend's house for a visit. They never made it home that day.

My mother had been having contractions that the doctor had thought were Braxton Hicks. When the contractions became unbearable, my grandmother sped to Riverside Hospital. I was born two hours later. My mother held me briefly before the nurses took me away.

Mom's hospital stay was unpleasant to say the least. She had a fever that had spiked during labor and wasn't permitted to see me. Her hospital room was semi-private, and the other patient's family was loud and unnerving for my pubescent, postpartum mother. One of the young males in attendance even crossed the room to hit on her!

In time, my mother could walk down to the nursery and look at me through the window. After two days she was well enough to hold me and nurse me. My mother said that she was awed by my beauty and that I was "perfect".

My mother had no relationship with my biological father at the time. She quickly got back into the routine of being a teenager, albeit a teenage mother. They were still living with Roger, and one weekend my grandmother and Roger went out of state for an Amway convention. Aunt Lynn and Mom decided it was a perfect opportunity to throw a summer party. They arranged to have a nice neighbor lady babysit for me.

My aunt invited her crush, a sixteen-year-old boy named Brett, who brought his friend, Kevin Henry. Kevin was supposed to hang out with Lynn's friend, but the night ended differently than as planned. There was drinking, loud music, the usual behavior one would expect out of teens when their parents were out of town. Later that night, my mother was walking barefoot in some tall grass and *stepped on a shard of broken glass*. Her foot was bleeding profusely, and Kevin came to the rescue and drove her to the local hospital: it was the beginning of a lifelong relationship.

Soon afterward, we moved out of Roger's place and into an old farmhouse on a hillside outside the small town of Mingo. I was about a year old by this time and my mother had re-entered Triad High School. When my grandmother got itchy feet and wanted to move yet again, my mother put her foot down. She was tired of moving and didn't want to switch high schools or be far away from Kevin, whom I was calling "Dad" by this time. My grandmother readily allowed my sixteen-year-old mother to move in with Kevin in order to ease some of her own financial strain.

My mother, Kevin, and I lived with his mom in their modest, three-bedroom, ranch style home for several months before we rented a trailer. Kevin had graduated while my mom had one year of school remaining. Mom attended high school while Kevin worked at an auto repair shop. The owner of the trailer decided to sell, which forced my mom to move back in with my grandmother, who was now living in Bellefontaine. At Christmas during my mother's junior year, Kevin proposed. The following spring, my mother graduated valedictorian of the Bellefontaine High School Class of 1982. She received a scholarship to attend Urbana College.

My parents were eighteen when they married. Both had exceptional work ethics and, though there were lean times and some struggles, they managed to keep things together. I consider their lives together a testament to hard work and commitment. I have many happy memories in my early childhood.

When I was four, my parents sat me down and told me that there would be a new baby in the family soon. They also explained that I had a different last name, but that my name would soon change to the same as theirs. I would no longer be an Evans, but a Henry: Kevin was going to adopt me. In the years to come, I gave no thought to the possibility that Kevin wasn't my biological father. I simply thought that I had a different last name because my parents weren't married when I was born.

A short time later, in 1984, we welcomed my brother, Nicholas. By that time, my dad had a steady job at Honda of America Manufacturing. Things were going well for my parents and we moved into a large, early 20th century house in the middle of our small town of North Lewisburg. It had five bedrooms, including a pink one for me, and a wrap-around porch. We would live there for the next ten years.

My parents worked hard to give Nicholas and me every advantage. When my mother wasn't doing volunteer work, she was shuttling my brother and me to our various extracurricular activities. My dad coached my sports teams as well. We had a swimming pool and a jungle gym, both provided by my youthful parents who easily kept up with two active children. I recall many memorable family vacations to the beach and other places.

Our family also included our beloved Golden Retriever, Oliver. Oliver loved to ride in the back of my dad's pick-up. He loved to play frisbee and was always by my side whenever I was upset or not feeling well. He was a faithful member of our home for thirteen years.

As I grew, I became a tomboy and enjoyed climbing trees, building forts, and playing various sports with the neighborhood boys. I was becoming quite an athlete, and my dad took notice and encouraged me.

I spent countless hours in the yard pitching the softball and catching high flies with him.

When I was about seven, my parents began attending the local Church of Christ. They became committed to their faith and changed their lives accordingly: no more house parties, no more liquor. They became active parishioners and our social activities revolved around the church. I enjoyed the social interaction that the church provided. I also loved singing during services. "Victory in Jesus" was the song that I always requested.

I was quite the social butterfly in and out of church and school. I am fairly certain that all of my elementary school report cards read, "Talks too much". I attended the same school, Triad, from kindergarten through my senior year as our county school system was quite small. While in the third grade, I met my first close friend at the local swimming pool. Her name was Anna. She was a girly-girl: into Barbies, painting her nails—all the things that I wasn't into. Ours was a classic case of "opposites attract". We would maintain a friendship for years to come.

At the age of eleven, I was still active in sports and I became acquainted with Triad's eighth grade girls' basketball coach, a woman by the name of Joyce Case. She offered me and a couple of my friends the opportunities to be "ball girls", or assistants to the team. Our jobs were varied: we worked out with the team, carried supplies, assisted the coach in whatever errands she needed. I loved every minute of it, especially traveling on the team bus. We would sing and chant, pumping ourselves up for the game. It was inspiring to be part of something bigger than myself, and the camaraderie was an experience I'll never forget. Being a "ball girl" also cemented my involvement in sports for the rest of my school years. I played basketball, volleyball, and softball. My decision to become an athlete, such a normal thing for a young person, did more to change the trajectory of my life than I could have imagined—then, anyway.

Revelations and the
"Father Apocalypse"

During my eighth-grade year, my parents invited me on a picnic to the Honda corporate park/playground. We had spent a lot of family time on this playground in years prior, and I was a little surprised that my parents only wanted me and not my brother to come along on this particular outing. I was excited to have some one-on-one time with my parents.

We sat on a checkered blanket on the ground next to a lake and had our picnic lunch. After a while, my mother said that they had something important they needed to share with me. I was then informed that Kevin was not my biological father. While a neighbor boy had once mentioned something about my dad not being my "real dad", I was still as shocked as anyone could imagine. I recall having so many questions: "What does my real dad look like?" "Does he live close?" "Is he nice?" "Will I ever meet him?"

There was also an immediate feeling of uncertainty, of being in limbo. My parents did their best to reassure me, although my mother had not spoken to the man since before my birth. She knew his name and where he had grown up. She explained to me how he had signed off on the adoption papers when I was four. Seeing my angst, my parents encouraged me to write him a letter—not to be mailed, but for cathartic purposes.

Kevin struggled especially hard that day: to him, I was his daughter. He wanted things to go on and be the same. That prospect was of course impossible—I was a thirteen-year-old girl who had just discovered she did not know her biological father. My life had experienced a seismic shift.

It was shortly after this revelation that we moved to a new home my parents had built in the country. The house was on ten acres, with apple trees, a pond, and a small forest. My dad eventually created a basketball court in our driveway so that I could practice. Our family began a new way of life, close to nature, with lots of space to roam and play.

In high school, I was a classic over-achiever, signing up for every club, sport and event available. I became quite the basketball star, averaging twenty-three points a game and breaking an all-time scoring record at my school with forty-three points in one game. I received All-Ohio honors in basketball and softball. I also excelled academically. Throughout my high school years, not only were my parents supportive, but Coach Joyce Case became an invaluable mentor, spurring me on to achievements in both sports and my studies.

Though I was a dream kid when it came to my achievements, I was also what my father called "boy crazy". My parents, being religious conservatives, did not allow me a great deal of freedom. They applied strict rules, making me choose between hanging out with friends or my boyfriend, limiting me to one social outing per week. Looking back, I did not have a lot of extra time but, in those moments, I felt like my parents were being too strict. They wanted to know where I was, at all times. Like a typical teen, I grew to resent my parents' rigidity when it came to my social life.

My mother became a little concerned about my behavior. When I turned sixteen, she was quick to remind me that I was the same age that she was when she had me. She showed me faith-based abstinence videos and lectured me on waiting until I was married to have sex. Though I can look back and understand that my parents wanted a different life for me at the time, at my adolescent age, I considered these lectures and reminders awkward and unnecessary.

In truth, I did want to spend all my free time with my boyfriends, who were usually athletes as well. I had two major romances during high school, Mike and Justin. When I was enamored, I gave up activities with my girlfriends and spent my free time with my beau.

Despite my resentment of my strict upbringing, my parents' whip-cracking paid off: I graduated with a 3.98 GPA and was Salutatorian of my senior class. My mother beamed at graduation: I had taken after her. I also received multiple scholarships and a full ride to Wright State University, where I was offered a walk-on position to play Division 1 softball.

The summer after graduation was my summer to be free of my parents' rules, or so I thought. I was soon reminded that, as long as I lived in their house, it was "their house, their rules". Of course, this did not sit well with my socially ambitious self. Communication at home was strained. Since the revelation that I wasn't really a Henry, my mother's and my relationship had become more distant. Being the introvert my mother was and still is, it was hard for the two of us to talk openly about sensitive topics. With all the teen angst and identity crises going on inside of me, I began to rebel.

One summer night, my friend Anna and I told our parents that we were spending the night at one another's houses, a convenient ruse when our plan was really to stay out all night. When we returned to Anna's house at six the next morning, there were notes stuck to virtually every door in the house: "Laurie, call your parents."

I was caught. There was nothing to do but…lie and try to get myself out of a bad situation. I told my parents that Anna and I had been asleep in her basement, unbeknownst to her family. Of course, my parents didn't buy a word of it and imposed even more restrictions. I, however, was having none of it and promptly moved in with Anna. Consequently, at the same time I also began the search for my biological father.

On the same day I moved in with Anna, I sat down in front of her computer and typed my real father's name in the search field on *MSN White Pages*. In a matter of seconds, I had a phone number.

I showed it to Anna. "Look what I found," I said.

"Now what are you going to do?" she asked.

We ran to her bedroom and dialed the number as we strained to hold both our ears to the receiver. A young girl's voice answered.

"Hello," I said, "may I please speak with C——?"

The girl replied that he was not in, but that I could call back later that evening.

Anna and I spent the next few hours waiting anxiously in her room. We rehearsed what I would say and discussed various scenarios of my future. Finally, it was time to call back.

"Hello," a man's voice answered.

I took a deep breath. "Hello, my name is Laurie Henry and my mother is Susan Evans. Are you who I think you are?"

I don't remember all the conversation after that, but he was surprised and happy about my call. He said he "didn't think this day would ever come" and that he was excited to meet me. We made plans to meet for dinner the next day at Damon's Grill. I was reeling from the overnight changes in my life and anxious for what lay ahead.

On the way to Damon's with Anna the next day, I was full of apprehension. Anna and I discussed all the possible scenarios that might result after this clandestine reunion. How would my parents take the news that I had met up with my real father? Would they be hurt or feel rejected? My intentions were good, I thought, and so I took courage knowing that.

Anna and I were escorted to a large table where I saw my biological father for the first time.

C—— was tall, with blond, graying hair and blue eyes. He reminded me of the actor Patrick Swayze. We were also introduced to his wife, along with his fourteen-year-old son and sixteen-year-old daughter. Things went smoothly and I soon relaxed. We soon discovered things we had in common: I learned that my biological father and I could touch our tongues to our noses. We had mutual favorite foods such as macaroni and cheese and egg sandwiches. Everyone was so welcoming. We enjoyed one another's company that evening and planned to continue growing our relationships.

As it turned out, I only stayed at Anna's house for two days. I soon moved back home with my parents—I guess one would say I was testing my limits as a young adult. I immediately told my parents that I had met up with C—— and his family. My folks were skeptical, but supportive. Of course, Kevin was fearful of being replaced. He had raised me since I was a baby and now this new person was in the picture. He had no idea if this would change our relationship. He had always dreamed of walking me down the aisle. Did my meeting C___ alter his future as well?

Summer flew by and soon it was time for me to be off to Wright State. I was excited for the freedom and flexibility that college life offered. Anna was my roommate, along with two other girls from a nearby town. I had no idea of the culture shock I was about to experience.

Finding Laurie

I had led a sheltered life growing up in North Lewisburg. I had never been exposed to other ethnicities outside of midwestern, white families. Because of my parents' strict religious faith and my dedication to sports, I had never been exposed to drinking or drugs, either.

As I mentioned, Anna was my roommate. My two other roommates were African-American. We shared a small dorm room, maybe 18'x20'. I immediately experienced a cultural divide. Hip-hop music blared at all hours and I had a strict study schedule. Anna promptly fell in with their constant socializing. I wasn't even sure if they went to class. Our dorm room was a center of activity morning and night. Boys even spent the night regularly. You can imagine my discomfort with couples engaging in various activities in the twin beds just feet from where I slept.

College softball also took up a lot of my time. We had multiple practices, study tables, and meetings and I had to attend them all. I had always been a serious student, and now I was surrounded by the college party life. Halfway through first semester, I phoned my parents, pleading with them to let me come home. College life was not what I had expected. My parents insisted that I give it a year. By the end of my first semester, all three of my roommates had not done well academically and one was expecting a baby.

After the first semester, things changed. Anna joined the Air Force and one of my other roommates dropped out. My pregnant roomie,

Shyra, stayed on. We got a new roommate, Ebony, who was very studious and did not like to party. Shyra began to take school more seriously. It was a much better balance, and the rest of the year turned out to be positive. I did like to socialize when time allowed, and I met many people my freshman year. Athletes tended to hang with other athletes, and I attended many baseball and basketball team parties.

My roommates also helped me discover my more feminine side. The tomboy look went away, and I learned to wear make-up and dresses. I had my hair highlighted and had it cut in layers. It didn't take long for me to realize that I liked my new look. Boys seemed to notice as well.

At the end of freshman year, I met a charismatic and cute athlete named Jeremy. He was also a fantastic dancer. Things got serious quickly, and parting for the summer proved to be painful—too painful. I was going home to my parents' place while Jeremy would be staying with friends. After a few days at home, I wanted out. I could no longer live by my parents' restrictions after so much freedom at school. In no time I was in my car and speeding towards Middletown, where Jeremy lived in an apartment with two other guys. I ended up moving in with them. That summer I was exposed to a whole new world: one that was dark and challenging.

Jeremy and his friends loved to go out dancing and partying and it was fun—at first. We went out almost every night. The drug "ecstasy" was prevalent around the club scene and in no time my friends were trying it. I was soon aware that I was not hanging around with a good crowd.

I started babysitting for money and took a regular job taking care of a girl named Zoey. She was my refuge from all the "crazy". I felt trapped by a world I knew was bad. Jeremy and I argued a lot. When school resumed, my stint in Middletown ended, and I moved back to Dayton into an apartment with three WSU softball players.

Jeremy and I separated at his insistence. I was in no way ready to let go and there were multiple, cloying, long-distance phone calls. I tried to convince him that I was all he needed. In turn, he played head games and manipulated me. I was in a horrible place. I had no self-esteem and my entire identity was wrapped up in being someone's girlfriend. After Jeremy broke up with me, I quit the softball team and threw myself into the club scene and partied constantly. I barely made a C average that fall. I took the following semester off, eventually losing my full ride scholarship.

My roommates did not understand me, and I did not understand them. I was seeking attention in all the wrong places and all I felt was alone. I had not saved any money, nor did I have any financial support. I called my mother, begging her to lend me money. She reminded me that we had an agreement that I was supposed to save some money for school over the summer. "You did not hold up your end of the bargain, so you are on your own," she said. When I told her I had no food, she was blunt: "You will have to figure something out." Talk about tough love!

I had to figure something out quickly. I was living on oatmeal and spaghetti while my roommates would have nice, sit-down dinners together. I was ostracized and in a terrible mental state. Then, I met Pamela.

Pamela and I were introduced one evening when I was out dancing at a night club. I was instantly drawn to this vivacious, brown-eyed blonde and her outgoing sense of humor. She was Irish, having moved to the states at thirteen. She had lost her brogue, but her Celtic cheekbones and broad, winning smile were gravitating. We connected immediately and at the end of the evening she gave me her pager number, insisting that I give her a call sometime. I paged her the following week and we got together at my place, shut in my room, sitting on my bed talking and laughing. I hadn't laughed so much in such a long time. We formed an instant friendship and began to hang out together constantly.

Pamela was a senior in high school at the time, though she was only one year younger than I. She had started school a year late in Ireland in order to attend the posh school her mom always dreamed of. I would pick her up from school and we'd go riding around in my '88 maroon Honda Civic. Pamela quickly became my first true BEST friend: a person whom I could trust with my most intimate secrets, who understood me and accepted me for all that I was. We connected on many levels as we had both experienced our share of turmoil and grief. One of the things I loved most about her were her stories of Ireland and her childhood. I never tired of hearing about how her "mum" would take her around Dublin on her father's bus, or how she would ride across the hills of County Dublin on horseback. I dreamed that one day she and I would go there, and she would show me her country.

My sophomore year of college was liberating in so many ways, but it also demonstrated that I was in no way centered or focused. I no longer had the rigid schedule of an athlete. I worked many jobs: waitressing, call centers, retail, car wash attendant, and some clerical work. I had thirteen different jobs that year, some lasting months, some weeks, and a few for half a day. I remember Pam coming into my apartment one day, asking me about my first day on a job. When I told her I had already quit, she threw up her hands in dismay, saying "Jesus, Laurie!"

Nowadays one would call my situation "survival mode". Halfway through the year, I did nail down a job at American Honda. I worked in the warehouse and was responsible for shipping parts to various body shops. I managed to hold down the job for several months, but in my spare time I was still hanging out with the wrong crowd. I didn't know it, but a huge change was on the horizon.

Our Platinum Wash Package: Foam Wax, Wheel Brite, and a Husband!

While working part-time as a cashier at a car wash, I met John, a tall, lanky brunette with deep brown eyes. He had come through with one of his friends to get a wash. We spoke briefly when he paid me: a casual flirtation, I suppose. After he and his friend left, I never gave it another thought.

A few months later I was at a party at a friend's house, and suddenly John walked in. "Hey, car wash girl," he said.

We chatted briefly and then, like before, he was gone. Weeks later, I ran into him again at a nightclub and we hung out and exchanged phone numbers. Two days later, he phoned me, asking if we could meet up.

I suggested a park near my place. I met him there and we sat on the swings, getting acquainted further, talking about our lives. He proceeded to tell me he was engaged to a woman he referred to as "Psycho". He had an eight-month-old daughter and was reluctant to leave the woman "because of the baby", or so he said. I instantly felt sorry for him. He seemed like such a nice guy and I thought he deserved to be happy. We ended our meeting with intentions of getting together again soon.

I met up with Pamela to tell her about the cute, sweet, unhappy guy I had met. Her reaction was one of shock. She apparently knew of him socially and wasted no time in telling me to stay away from him, that he was bad news. I didn't listen. Years later, Pamela would recall watching me walk away with John after one of our social gatherings. "I had such a feeling of dread," she said.

I lapped up the attention John gave me like a starved kitten. In turn, I wanted to help him out of his terrible situation. It wasn't long before he moved in with me. My roommates had gone home for the summer, so I had plenty of room in my apartment. On the morning after his first night at my place, he went outside to find his tires slashed, courtesy of "Psycho". He couldn't make it to work and was fired as a result. Rather than see this as the red flag it was, my heart caved with sympathy.

In the meantime, my parents were far from happy with me. I had not called them in weeks, was behind on my car payments, and was avoiding various other responsibilities. It turned out neither John nor I was working, so we decided to escape the drama and road trip to Pennsylvania to see my biological father, who was there on a job site at the time.

We spent a few fun-filled days there before returning to Dayton and reality. We had to make a decision, as my roommates had moved out and John and I could not afford the three-bedroom townhouse. My parents said I could move home with them, but C___ offered to let John and me move in with his family. Of course, that was a no-brainer: I wasn't going anywhere without John, who by this time I had known for a total of one month.

My parents immediately took away my car since I wasn't making my agreed portion of the payments. When John and I arrived at our new home in London, Ohio, the family reunion was a happy one at first. We all hung out, partied, lived our lives together—but things went downhill quickly.

I had found a job as a nanny for a family friend for a hundred dollars a week. John worked at a local auto body shop. Meanwhile, we shared a room with my sixteen-year-old half-sister. My stepmom's brother also lived with us. Things were crowded and chaotic. There was lots of drama among various people, myself included.

Finally, everyone had had enough. John and I needed to get out. I phoned my Uncle Bob's wife, Angela, and explained my dilemma. After a long phone call, she and Bob, my mother's brother, agreed to take us in. They had three children of their own! We had to sleep on the sofa. I was grateful to them both.

After the move to my uncle's in North Lewisburg, John and I managed to get temp jobs at a warehouse where my Aunt Lynn worked. Eventually, we both joined the National Guard in attempt to do something with our lives. I worked and saved enough money to get my car back. It was about this time that John was arrested for stealing cigarettes and spent two days in jail. My uncle was furious. He told me I could stay, but John had to go. John was about to be deployed, so I needed only a quick fix for living arrangements.

I had lost my scholarship at Wright State and begun attending classes at a community college where I met Kenzie, a single mom who lived with her daughter. We would spend our class breaks together in the school cafeteria getting to know one another. We formed an instant friendship. One day, we met up in our usual spot at school and I told her about my dilemma. She offered to let John and me stay with her at her place in Xenia.

Soon after, John was sent to Army basic training at Fort Jackson, South Carolina and I stayed behind with Kenzie and her daughter. There was a Frisch's Big Boy right across the street from Kenzie's, so I took a waitressing job there. I went to work and school and hung out with Kenzie; occasionally, John's daughter came to stay with me. John and I wrote letters back and forth. I felt like my life was back on track. I was happy.

John graduated from basic with flying colors. Kenzie and I planned a road trip to South Carolina for graduation. We took her young daughter along. When we arrived and I saw John for the first time in so many weeks, it was a happy reunion. He looked better than ever and exuded a confidence I'd never seen before. He was excited for his new career. It killed me to have to say goodbye and leave him there.

Not long after Kenzie and I returned to Ohio, John called me. By this time we had been dating seven months. My birthday was coming up, and he encouraged me to buy a ring: an engagement ring. He instructed me to take some money out of his account and go pick out the ring I wanted. I was beyond excited—but first, I had to tell my parents.

When I phoned home and told my mother the news, she was less than excited. She didn't say much at first, but she did take me out to lunch to voice her concerns. Gradually, I got the idea she wasn't totally against my engagement. I was twenty-one and I had a job and was going to school. She soon realized that I was determined, and she began planning a wedding.

After the phone call, it was time to go shopping. John had eight-hundred dollars in his bank account, so I wasn't exactly going shopping for the Hope Diamond. Pamela went with me and we picked out a modest, 1/3 carat diamond in a white gold setting for four hundred dollars. Then, we shared the news with her mother, Edel, who was far from happy with my decision and thought I was making a huge mistake.

We set a date for August, when John would return home. My mother found a venue after deciding that she would make all the food for the event. She had given me a budget of two thousand dollars—not much for a wedding by today's standards. Mom rented tents and borrowed flowers. She also bought my dress. My biological father paid for the hairdresser, the photographer, and our honeymoon. I was excited for the big day.

In the middle of all the wedding plans, one of John's friends, Clint, reached out to me and said he wanted to share something with me. It turned out that John had not only confessed but bragged to him that he had been unfaithful to me throughout our relationship, including an interlude with "Psycho" and—to my shock—a close family member! I was in utter disbelief. The conversation went on until finally this "friend" tried to hit on me! I was a total mess and didn't know what to believe.

When I finally called John, he told me that his friend had lied, that he only wanted to break us up. He reassured me that none of those things had happened, and of course, I believed him. I wanted to believe him, *had* to believe him—after all, my mother had the wedding plans all in order and the invitations were already in the mail.

In retrospect, emotionally I was a prime target for a malignant narcissist. Things weren't going to get any easier any time soon.

Wedding Bell Blues

We were married in August at a log cabin in Mingo, Ohio. The cabin sat on a lake and the surrounding view was gorgeous. My mom planned a beautiful wedding with all our close friends and family in attendance. Pamela, Kenzie, and my half-sister Karen were my bridesmaids. My biological father was a groomsman while my dad, Kevin, walked me down the aisle. After the reception, Aunt Lynn hosted an after-party at her country house. It was a perfect day. John and I returned to the cabin for our wedding night. I tried to ignore my gut feeling that I had just made a huge mistake. I cared too much about my mother's hard work and about what our friends might think.

John and I moved from Xenia to London, Ohio after he received a job offer. We got our very own apartment. He worked at the autobody shop where he had previously worked while I found a clerical job. We had joint custody of his fifteen-month-old daughter and settled in to making a family life. Shortly after we moved to London, Pamela began dating my half-sister's ex-boyfriend, Josh. This was great for me, because it meant that I would see more of Pamela. Unfortunately, my sister still harbored feelings for Josh and she began making waves, so to speak. It was about this same time that I got a call from my stepmom, asking me to come over to my bio-father's house for "a talk". Somehow, I knew it wasn't going to be good.

I picked up Pamela and she went with me. When we arrived at the house we were promptly surrounded by C____, my stepmom, and my half-sister. As I sat on a brown footstool in the living room, my family informed us that John had recently tried to seduce my sister and she refused him. C____ suggested that John needed "some help".

I felt like I'd been punched in the stomach. I'd been married for a total of one month. Pamela and I left the house and began looking for John. After searching for over an hour, we gave up and returned to my apartment, where John was just pulling into the driveway. When I confronted him, he flew into a rage and insisted that we go to my biological father's house. I desperately wanted to believe my husband, so I acquiesced. When we arrived, it was nothing but a huge screaming match with John calling my family "liars" and a few other choice names.

I cried myself to sleep that night and then lay in bed the entire day afterward. I needed a break, time away, to think. I went for a drive with John and tried to explain my feelings. Things became heated and he asked me to stop the car. Before I could pull over, he jumped out of the car and out of nowhere produced a box cutter and slashed his wrist, saying that he didn't want to live without me. I rushed him to the emergency room where, after he was treated, he was evaluated by a psychologist. The psychologist cautioned me not to leave John alone while he was in this state. What could I do?

I kept the entire incident under wraps and tried to cope. I was so ashamed of everything. I struggled to keep up appearances while I was miserable inside. Dealing with John became more challenging than ever. He lied about the most ridiculous things. Once, he told a friend that a scar he had was "from being shot in the war". It was actually a surgical scar from when he had an in-grown hair removed! I would find slips of paper with women's phone numbers in his pants pockets, but he would have "no idea" how they got there.

John's manic behavior had me walking on eggshells. He would cry and make me feel guilty for all his wrongdoings. Once, I attempted to leave him and he tossed my clothes off the balcony and punched holes in the wall. The next minute, he was Prince Charming. We were living paycheck to paycheck while I tried to think of a way to help my husband and make my marriage last.

#

One good thing that happened during this dismal time was that I took a job at an upscale family-owned restaurant in Dublin, Ohio called LaScala. My neighbor Amanda worked there, and she talked me into applying. I was hired and instantly loved it. I was exposed to new friendships and a new way of life. My coworkers were great. And, I finally had a steady income.

John decided he would go full time into the military instead of the National Guard. I ended my career with the Guard in turn. John was deployed to Washington D.C. At the same time, his daughter came to live with us full time. With John deployed, I was a parent on my own. His daughter and I moved in with my folks for a month or so before I rented an apartment in Fairborn and re-enrolled at Wright State.

John and I spoke often on the phone, but there were many nights he didn't call. When I would call him, he was usually in a bar somewhere, drinking and partying with his buddies. I worried constantly about what he was doing and whom he was with. I couldn't dwell on it: I had his child to contend with. Her mother had visitation rights, and I was constantly on the phone with child services. I had to grow up overnight and care for a child who didn't belong to me and whose father didn't love me. My friends and co-workers at LaScala were a great support at the time.

On my 24th birthday, John came home and surprised me with an evening out with friends. He bought me a party dress and hired a limo to drive about ten of us out on the town. After an evening of drinking and dancing, we stopped at a gas station for a brief pit stop. I went to the bathroom and when I came out, everyone was in the gas station buying drinks and snacks. I went out to the limo alone and found John's phone ringing on the back seat. I picked it up and answered.

"Hello," I said.

"Is John there?" a girl's voice asked.

"Yes, he is," I replied. "Who's calling?"

"His girlfriend."

"How nice to meet you," I said. "This is John's wife."

John came back to the limo and saw me on his phone. His face turned white: he knew. The forty-five-minute ride home was a nightmare. We argued in front of our friends and of course he denied everything. I spent a sleepless night, wondering what I was going to do.

The next morning, I woke up early. John was sound asleep, so I quietly removed his phone from his pants pocket and went outside. I called the number from the night before and his "girlfriend" answered. We had a long talk: she even gave me her voicemail code so I could listen to all of John's voicemails to her. I thought I would vomit when I heard him calling her baby and saying he loved her.

When John woke up, he had a litany of excuses. He tried to say it was all a lie and the girl was crazy, but the next minute he tried to justify the relationship, saying he was lonely. I was furious as I listened to his lies. I was taking care of his child while he was out screwing around! I was nothing but a babysitter. Sadly, I wasn't angry enough to walk away.

John was deployed, and I threw myself into work and classes. I also started seeing a therapist, who advised me to work out, find some new friends, and do things that made me happy. I did everything the therapist challenged me to do. I even found a new friend, Abigail, a girl in my Spanish class.

Pamela had been avoiding me because she was fed up with John's behavior and my denial. Who could blame her? But I missed her and needed someone to hang out with. Abigail was a welcome addition to my list of friends. Abigail was one of seven children. A fine art major, she was an athletic and studious brunette of Irish/Italian descent who was also a kind and compassionate person. She sewed, knitted, cooked amazing food and was the most well-rounded person I had ever met at the time. We had both struggled with relationships but chose not to talk about them much. Instead, we took bike rides, rollerbladed, and studied together. Abigail didn't judge me over John, and she was supportive of me saving my marriage. We attended church regularly as well. Abigail and I made all sorts of plans. We had fun together—and I badly needed some fun in my life.

John came home for a weekend visit and we spent some quality time together. Things went smoothly—so smoothly that a month later I discovered I was pregnant! When I told John, he was somewhat shocked but did not appear to be disappointed in any way. His immediate reaction was to phone his mother.

Though a baby hadn't been in my immediate plans, I made the best of it and started taking good care of myself. Abigail was happy for me. We went to a Christian concert with my parents, who were in their forties at the time, and I told them the news. They were thrilled to be grandparents. My happiness was short-lived, however, when soon afterward I found out that John was being dishonorably discharged from the Army. I found myself five months pregnant with an unemployed husband and no medical benefits. We had to live on the money I made at LaScala.

John was supposed to be looking for a job, but he spent his time hanging out with friends. Meanwhile, I took a second job at a bank while I continued going to school full-time and working at LaScala. I ran a 5K. I tried to focus on giving my baby a good life and not think about everything else.

John finally got a job as a security guard working third shift. This meant that we didn't see each other much. I began keeping a pregnancy journal, writing down my thoughts and concerns at the time. I loved the idea of having my own little baby but having a baby with John in my life looked less and less promising. I didn't want my child growing up in a tumultuous household. Thankfully, Abigail, Pamela, my LaScala friends, and my family were great support. Abigail would bring me granola bars during class to make sure I was eating. I didn't feel nearly as alone as I had in the past.

The lease was up on our apartment, so we took a three-bedroom house in Xenia, Ohio. I was eight months pregnant, moving boxes and furniture into my new house. Pamela and I would load up her white Ford Explorer time and time again to move everything. She was a huge help. Needless to say, John was not. Eventually, my dad showed up with his truck and forced John to help move the last few large items.

After we got settled into the house, my last month of pregnancy was a rush of activity. I had four baby showers! John and I came up with the name Sofia Marie. We chose the Italian spelling of Sofia (like Sofia Loren). Marie was my mother's middle name. I was anxious to become a mother, but uncertain of the future.

My First "Emerald Isle"

A few weeks after Sofia was born, Pamela and I, along with the baby, were hanging by the pool at her apartment complex. She was living with her boyfriend Josh at the time and working on her MBA. I confided in her that I was miserable and that the constant lies from John, as well as the endless infidelities, were too much for me to take. Pamela suggested that Sofia and I join my parents on their upcoming trip to the Outer Banks. They had rented a house on Emerald Isle, North Carolina, along with several other relatives, but had indicated earlier that they were taking their bikes, so they had no room for other passengers. Pamela insisted that I needed a vacation, a break from the chaos with John, and that I should try to persuade my parents somehow.

Shortly after our talk, I drove to my Aunt Lynn's. She lived in a beautiful old 19th century brick farmhouse in rural Ohio. Aunt Lynn had been my moral support on many occasions, and now I needed her more than ever. My parents were not always the most communicative when it came to emotions, and I think they felt that now that I was married and had a child, I needed to stand on my own two feet. Aunt Lynn helped persuade my parents to make room for their daughter and grandchild as they "needed time away". My grandfather agreed to pick up my part of the tab, and my parents relented and said they could rent bikes instead. Little six-week-old Sofia and I were going on a much-needed vacation!

When we arrived on Emerald Isle, my extended family was excited to meet the new family member. Sofia was the center of attention the entire trip. We spent time at the beach, watched fireworks, checked out the Wright Brothers Memorial and enjoyed wonderful family dinners. In the evening, I would go to our upstairs bedroom and try to call my husband. Sometimes he answered, but most of the time it went to voicemail. What few conversations I managed to have with him were perfunctory and distant. My heart was breaking. I would listen to the rest of my family downstairs, laughing and having a great time while I was unhappy and uncertain of my future.

I had said nothing of John's abuse or any of our problems because I didn't want my parents to dislike him. I held all my frustrations inside and would retreat to my room with the baby and just hold her close, promising her I would be the best mother I could, no matter what. Of course, I stayed in touch with Pam the whole time I was in North Carolina. She was worried about me and fed up with my husband's infantile and irresponsible behavior. She also reminded me that I wielded all the power: because John was frivolous with money, his credit was in the toilet and the bills were all in my name—including his cell phone. On the day I was to return home with my parents, I called the cell service and shut off his phone in an attempt to get his attention.

As Sofia and I rode along in the mid-section of my father's Honda Pilot, my mind raced with apprehension and dread. Whatever was waiting for me at home, it couldn't be good. I became so upset I finally broke down and told my parents everything. I told them about the affairs, our money problems, John's vague excuses about not receiving a paycheck on time, and my fears for Sofia's and my futures.

My parents were shocked. They had been unaware of the severity of our problems as a young married couple. They told me they were sorry, but nothing more was said. Moments later they were talking about how much they had enjoyed the trip. I think they were waiting to get home to discuss their daughter's issues in private. Later, I found out they were secretly relieved and hoping that John would be out of our lives. They felt that Sofia and I had a better chance without him.

I suddenly remembered the joint bank account that John and I shared. I dialed the bank's automated line to check the balances: "Checking Balance: Zero dollars; Savings Balance: Zero dollars". He had cleaned them out. I was devastated. How could he abandon his wife and child and leave them with no money for groceries, diapers, whatever? The rest of the car ride home was a grueling nightmare, with my parents' stoic demeanors and me in a state of panic.

When we arrived at my parents' house, they asked me what I intended to do. I told them that I was going to drive home and salvage whatever I could of my life. I strapped Sofia in her car seat and off we went. Pamela and her boyfriend Josh offered to meet me at my place, just in case John was there and things got hot. They were there when I arrived. Josh and Pam insisted that Sofia and I stay the night at their place, in case John came home unannounced. Josh also changed the locks on our house so that John could not take any of our things.

The next morning, I woke up on Josh and Pam's sofa, grateful for such good friends but still terrified. I phoned Jenny, John's mother, and told her what had happened. She sympathized with me, saying that she knew that her son was capable of bad behavior but that she never thought he would take it this far. She had not heard from him but told me that if Sofia and I needed anything, to call her—as if I wasn't already in immediate need! My baby and I were sleeping on a friend's sofa! My fate was sealed: it was off to Greene County Job and Family Services to apply for welfare.

Sofia and I sat in the crowded waiting area until I met with my case worker, a kind woman named Ruth. She patiently listened as I told her my problems and by the end of our conversation had given me some hope. I told her that I had always worked and was completing my education. I had only come there as a last resort. She understood and reassured me that that was what Family Services was for. I found that I qualified for

Medicaid, food stamps, and financial assistance. At least I knew my baby would have medical care and not go hungry. Feeling a small sense of relief, I returned to Pamela and Josh's place.

When a woman knows she's entering a new phase in life, she often yearns for a physical transformation to coincide with her external changes. I asked Pamela if she would cut my hair—an ominous prospect since she had no professional experience. We sat in the garage amid storage boxes while she trimmed my long tresses, giving my hair layers and framing my features. It wasn't a stellar cut, but when she was finished I felt lighter, inside and out.

Going home to live with my parents was not an option as far as I was concerned. I resolved to find a way to put a roof over my and Sofia's heads. Since Sofia was only seven weeks old, I was still on maternity leave from my jobs at LaScala and the local Credit Union, where I had worked since I was seven months' pregnant. I phoned my boss, Brian, at LaScala and he added me back to the weekend schedule immediately. My parents and Aunt Lynn agreed to rotate childcare while I worked. I then went to the Credit Union and, after allowing all my former co-workers to meet Sofia, spoke with my supervisor. I tearfully explained that I was going to have to leave my job because I couldn't afford the additional childcare money it would take for me to work there. She was sympathetic and wished Sofia and me well.

Sofia and I returned to the house John and I had rented. There was still no sign of him. A few days later, Sofia's step-great grandmother, "Baca" as everyone called her, got in contact with me. Jenny had apparently gotten the word out to the family about our situation. "Baca" invited Sofia and me to meet her for breakfast at Bob Evans the following day. I had only met her a couple of times, so the phone call was a bit of a shock. She said she had a baby gift for me and was looking forward to meeting Sofia.

Baca was in her sixties, retired from General Motors, and was one of those women who was always "put together"—hair coiffed like she had just left the salon and her nails freshly lacquered. She was an assertive woman with the best sense of humor. We sat at a table next to the window, getting reacquainted as we looked out on a warm summer morning.

"How are you and the baby doing?" she asked me.

"Ok, considering the circumstances," I replied. "I have no idea where John is, and I haven't heard from him in over a week."

"Baca" was thoughtful before she replied. "You know, when my daughters and I saw you at the baby shower, we couldn't understand how John had married someone like you. You are a good person, you are good with his daughter. During the shower, John made himself the center of attention while you cared for his child! Then, we saw you, nine months' pregnant and carrying boxes while he sat on his high horse!"

I told Baca that when I took my vows, I intended to stay married forever. I hoped to work things out. To my surprise, she had her own ideas.

"You can do better. You deserve better. Do not go back to him, do you understand me? Be strong!"

At the end of our meeting, she gave me some money that the family had pulled together for me and Sofia. I was overwhelmed with her kindness and promised I would stay in touch.

I left that meeting feeling better than I had in days. At least I knew that not everyone was judging me as a failure in my marriage. I had a little money, I was going back to work, and it looked like my baby and I would not be out in the street.

As luck or fate would have it, one of my college friends, Michelle, was going through a bad break-up. We shared our mutual stories and began hanging out. She ended up staying at my place frequently and was a great companion and a huge help with Sofia.

My mom's youngest sister, Emily, who was four years younger than I, visited us. Emily was great with Sofia and was a joy to have around. During one of her visits, we created a pink scrapbook of Sofia's first thirty days, a treasured memory that will always be a reminder of where Sofia's and my journey began.

It was also during this time that Pam and Josh went on a European vacation. When they returned, Pam told me of a vision she had during their travels. She was watching several young couples boarding a yacht on the Mediterranean Sea. She instantly envisioned me living that life and said that the feeling was overwhelming. I had never seen a yacht—let alone been to Europe. I had no idea at the time that dreaming about a boat could signify a new beginning on the horizon—or a new romance.

Of course, things couldn't stay on the upswing forever. Not only was my husband nowhere to be found, but debt collectors were calling. John's 2002 Honda Civic was in my name as well, and the payments were behind. The debt collectors obviously didn't care that I had no idea where the car was and had no money to make a payment because my jerk husband took all my money. It was time to find John and make him face reality.

I phoned a friend of John's and begged him to get in contact with him. I explained the situation, knowing that he probably wouldn't give out John's number, so I just asked him to relay the information about the car. A short time later, Michelle, Sofia, and I were hanging at my place when my cell phone rang: "Unknown Caller". My stomach was in knots as I answered the call. I had resolved to not discuss any of John's recent indiscretions and dishonesty and simply focus on the issue at hand. I informed him that I had contacted a loan agency in Columbus that specialized in loans for people with bad credit. John agreed to meet me the next day and drive to Columbus.

I met John at a Wal-Mart and he got in my car. As we headed for Columbus, we made small talk, but I was incredulous at his detachment and his blasé attitude, as if the past few weeks had never happened. Whenever I discussed Sofia, telling him that she was beginning to smile or any such other baby updates, he became uncomfortable and changed the subject. I decided to share my new favorite song with him and popped in a Shania Twain CD. I forwarded to a song called "Nah".

"Though I might begin/ by fillin' you in/ In case you didn't already know/ I'll never forget how you got up and left/ In fact it was downright pretty low."

In no time, John was in tears. He begged forgiveness, saying he never meant to hurt me or Sofia and that he cared about us. As he puked excuses, I felt myself growing stronger and stronger. Though I felt pity for him, I thought of "Baca's" words.

"It was good while it lasted. Now, I'm past it," I sang along with the song.

John said he wanted to take care of his responsibilities and that he would give me fifty dollars a week until we could "establish child support". I had seen enough of his behavior with his other child to not put too much stock in his promises.

Not surprisingly, John didn't get the car loan. We drove back to Columbus, discussing our separation and other necessary details. At times our words grew heated, but we managed to rein them in. When I left him in the parking lot at Wal-Mart, I knew I could do this thing without him. Whatever help I got from him would just be windfall. It was all on me.

"Excuse Me, Your Wife is Waiting"
(for Child Support)

On a sunny September day, a few days before classes started, I was with Pamela on the Wright State campus. We passed the Legal Services office and I wondered if they might be able to assist me with my divorce. I had been told by a law firm in Dayton that divorcing my husband would cost me two thousand dollars. When I paid my tuition, there was a seven-dollar fee attached for "legal services". Until that day, I never understood the reason, nor the tremendous value of that fee.

I spoke to the school attorney named Sam, and he agreed to assist me in drawing up my dissolution agreement. I met with John on our fourth wedding anniversary, and he signed the papers. The attorney filed the papers and a court date was set for January 6th, 2006.

I went on attending classes, working at LaScala, and trying to support my daughter and I. Sofia and I bonded as any mother and child should. She was the center of my world, and every effort I made to advance myself was for her sake.

One of the classes I took at this time was called "The Psychology of Incarceration". The professor had developed the class initially for prisoners who were about to exit the prison system. It was designed to help them reintegrate into society. While in prison, they had to live in survival mode. Transitioning back into the everyday world was challenging.

Ironically, I found their experience very similar to my life during my marriage. The coursework was invaluable in understanding myself and my motivations in a whole new way.

It was also during this time that Pamela's and my communications professor, Dr. Morgan, recommended that we read *Excuse Me, Your Life is Waiting*. The book discussed visualizing what one wanted and sending positive thoughts into the universe. I began to focus on positive thoughts creating positive outcomes. I worked with Dr. Morgan to come up with ideas on my final project on positivity. I was hooked on these life-changing concepts.

In Dr. Morgan's class, I sat next to a friendly guy named Adam. One day, during class, he asked me if I knew who Paul McCartney was. Even now I am embarrassed to write that I did not know. Adam handed me a CD, and said that if I liked the music, that he had tickets to see McCartney in concert the following month.

"You are welcome to come along," he said.

I met Adam and his family at a pizzeria in Columbus on the night of the concert. Let me say that the energy in the stadium that night was like nothing I had ever experienced. I was launched into a much larger music culture spectrum than singing hymns in church. As I watched clips on a huge screen of Paul's career with the Beatles and his later solo career, as I listened to Paul play piano, guitar, and sing for two hours, I was inspired by a life of phenomenal accomplishment.

I graduated with a BA in Communications from Wright State in November of 2005. Sofia sat with my parents as I walked up the aisle to get my diploma. With the challenges of an early marriage and single motherhood, it had taken me six years to finish a four-year degree—but I had made it. Now, it was time to get a "real" job.

I had not narrowed down exactly what I wanted to do as far as a career. I visited with my "Psychology of Incarceration" teacher and he suggested that I volunteer somewhere to get some experience that might direct me in a desirable path. The next weekend, I began volunteering at a local juvenile jail. I spent time in the classrooms with the students, and I found the work rewarding.

The holidays were approaching, and it would be Sofia's first Christmas. One day, Pam was at my place. She looked around my apartment and asked, "Where are your Christmas decorations?"

I told her that Sofia and I planned to be at my parents for Christmas, so I wasn't going to bother. Pamela promptly went out and bought me a lighted, miniature tree. She wanted me to have some Christmas spirit in my own home. I loved the warm ambience the tree gave to my modest rental. Since John's departure, I had not felt at home there until that moment.

Sofia and I spent the night of Christmas Eve at my parents' home, and the following day celebrated with the whole family. I was looking forward to a new year and a new beginning.

# #

Up until the time of our divorce hearing, I had little contact with John, and little support. He had not inquired about Sofia's welfare, nor had he asked to spend any time with her. I was relieved by the latter, as I did not want to worry about my baby's safety. I dreaded the idea of court-granted visitation with a father who had no real interest in his child.

Pamela and I arrived at the Green County courthouse on a cold gray January morning. The irony was not lost on me that I was driving the same car that John and I had taken to the hospital the day of Sofia's birth. My nerves were raw, and I was so grateful for Pamela's presence.

We parked in front of the courthouse fifteen minutes before the appointed time. Pamela and I were sitting in the car, talking about the future, when there was a loud *bang-bang-bang!* We nearly jumped out of our skins. John had appeared out of nowhere and pounded on the driver's side window. He stood outside, glaring at the two of us.

"Let's go!" he ordered.

We got out of the car after Pamela offered a few choice words of her own. As we followed John into the courthouse, with several security personnel standing nearby, he called over his shoulder angrily: "You're not supposed to bring your friends to these types of things!"

Pamela had heard enough. "Well, John, I'm surprised you don't have your pregnant girlfriend with you!"

One of the officers told John to shut his mouth and to go have a seat.

Things are off to a wonderful start, I thought. I was somewhat calmer when I located my attorney in the waiting area.

Once we were in the hearing room, the judge quickly went over the documents and asked if there were any discrepancies or considerations.

"The only thing I do not agree with is supervised visitation with my daughter," John said.

The judge, a short, bespectacled man in his sixties with a calm disposition, looked at John directly. "Mister _____, how many times have you seen your daughter since she was born? Are you currently supporting her financially? Do you have a crib? A car seat? Have you purchased diapers or formula?"

Clearly, this wasn't this judge's first rodeo.

John answered in a string of sheepish negatives before he started to offer excuses. The judge promptly cut him off. The supervised visits would stand until John had proven that he could exercise the current rights he was granted.

I think I took my first breath of the entire day at that moment. I had been petrified of sending Sofia off with my erratic and unstable husband. I owed that judge flowers or a free dinner at LaScala. Pamela and I left the courthouse savoring my victory.

The lease was up on the rental house in Xenia and I was ready for a change. I wanted to rid my life of any residuals that reminded me of my ex. I was a single mother with lousy credit, so I was fearful of my options. John's mom, Jenny, always a guardian angel, mentioned that she had seen a "For Rent" sign on a house in Fairborn and had taken down the number. I phoned right away and spoke to the landlord, a woman named Rita. In no time, Sofia and I were off to check out the house.

The place was a disaster: black stains on the carpet, filth everywhere, and an indescribable odor. I did like the layout: it had two bedrooms, a laundry room as well as a garage and a small yard. I made a deal with Rita on the rent, with the promise that I would make drastic improvements to the place. Sofia and I were beginning afresh.

It was also during this time that my personal life began to evolve. Jack was Pamela's best "guy friend". They had been friends for several years, but I had never met him. Pam introduced us and we started hanging out.

Jack was a ruggedly handsome, outdoors-type with kind blue eyes and a broad smile. In contrast to his classic masculine looks was his compassionate demeanor: he was just enough of a mama's boy to be attractive. Sadly, he had experienced a horrible tragedy some years before, when he was involved in a car crash where his girlfriend was killed. Jack had suffered from depression and survivor's guilt ever since. I was the first girl in whom he had showed interest since the accident. I tried to be patient and understanding.

Jack was a generous person and was a huge help with my new place. He would come over and we would have late-night painting parties as we listened to Dave Matthews Band and ate pizza. The new place quickly transformed into a warm and cozy home.

Not long after I had moved into the place in Fairborn, I began receiving calls from debt collectors: John had defaulted on the car payments. Though I was not surprised, it wasn't something that I relished having to attend to. When I finally contacted John after several tries, he informed me that the car had a broken axle and was sitting in the parking lot of his apartment complex. I immediately phoned the collection agency and they asked that I determine the car's location.

I went to John's apartment complex and waited for the "repo man" to arrive. As I sat there in my car, an old, battered pick-up pulled into the parking lot: John was in the passenger seat and exited the truck, immediately approaching my car. I told him that I was there to take back the car.

John immediately became agitated. "Ok, I'll give you the keys, but can you please wait across the street? My girlfriend is on her way home and I don't want her to know that you are here."

Same old games. Not once did he inquire about Sofia.

I called Pamela and asked her to join me while I waited. As we sat there, talking and biding our time, another car pulled in and a woman and a young girl got out and went inside the building. I was overcome with resentment and pity at the same time.

When the repo man arrived, I gave him the keys: another bridge burned. I went home feeling sad, but a little more weightless.

How to Be a Blank Slate

Sofia and I settled into our happy family routine. My parents and Aunt Lynn were the best childcare a young mother could ask for. There was also Baca, who would invite us over to her house, along with the rest of her grandchildren. The kids would swim in her pond, ride around in her golf cart, and when the weather was bad Baca would let them convert her living room into a playground. Seeing Baca play in one of the kids' makeshift "forts" is a memory I'll never forget. She was the source of many happy days for me and my daughter.

In early 2006, at one of my child support meetings, I noticed a job posting for a Youth Works Case Manager. It was a six-month position that paid twelve dollars an hour—I decided to go for it. In no time I was called for an interview and promptly hired.

I ended up loving this job. Little did I know, though, being the country girl I was, that I would be visiting some impoverished, crime-ridden urban areas around Dayton. My job was to help underprivileged youth find summer employment, as well as to teach and tutor life skills and administer academic testing. I also recruited companies to sponsor this government-funded program and hire our candidates.

Meeting the families in this process opened my eyes to the many challenges that people have. It made me appreciate my own situation, but also taught me a lot about common human frailties. Most people I met while I worked for Family Services were kind, wonderful folks, from the families to the volunteers to the other social workers. I experienced a connectivity because of my own need for government assistance. The job broadened my personal horizons and made me reconsider my career options. When the position ended in August, I was sad. I picked up more shifts at LaScala—but I had several new ideas about where my life was headed.

It was also in August of that year that I got an unexpected phone call from John.

"You need to tell the judge that you don't want anything from me," he said after a terse greeting.

When I asked him what he meant, John told me that he was about to go to jail for non-payment of child support. I couldn't believe it: he was asking me to tell a judge that I didn't want the child support that I was legally entitled to and wasn't receiving. The audacity was mind-boggling.

I immediately told him that I would do no such thing, and then I added something: *"If someday in the future I remarry and my new husband wants to adopt Sofia, then I'll consider your offer."*

#

I was still trying to focus on a career path, and my friend Abbie from Youth Works, who taught middle school, suggested that I might look into becoming a teacher. With my communications degree, I had limited options, so I began taking prerequisite masters' courses at a local community college, with plans to attend Wright State later.

In the meantime, my relationship with Jack was on-again, off-again. I determined that his ongoing grief was a barrier to commitment. I tried to understand his past and be sympathetic, but I needed more. When I would discuss a committed relationship, he would only say "Do we need to have a label?" I elected to give him his space.

In the end, Jack's inability to commit did me a favor. I became more self-reliant and determined. Sofia had to come first, and it was my job and my job only to see that she had the life she deserved. Her happiness, along with my own, would be the constructs of my own independent efforts.

Seven months after I left Youth Works, I got a job as a Medicaid caseworker. Again, I was making twelve dollars an hour, but I had benefits, vacation time, and a retirement plan, not to mention some wonderful co-workers. My life took on an air of stability I had never experienced. As I began helping others with their government assistance, I was able to end my own reliance on food stamps and other aid. I felt like I was giving back on so many levels. Of course, I still had to work at LaScala to make up for the deficit in income. Having a full-time job meant that I would have to put Sofia in daycare, and the cost was astronomical in relationship to what I earned. But things were truly looking up!

Becoming a Medicaid caseworker was a significant milestone in my life. For one thing, I learned that every person has a different story. Sometimes I could relate through my own personal history; other times, I was overwhelmed by the challenges I observed. I learned not to be so quick to paint people with a broad brush.

My co-workers were another enriching aspect of my new vocation. Arlene, a woman from NY in her sixties, became a close confidant. We were from totally different backgrounds, both culturally and ethnically, but we had so much in common in the ways we focused on positivism. Another woman, Ann, was from India. She opened my eyes to a new culture, introducing me to the food and traditions of her homeland. Interestingly, she took me on tours of the city I was now calling home, and I got to see things for the first time, yet through an outsider's eyes. We went to the Dayton Art Institute, the Wright Brothers' bicycle shop, and visited various museums and monuments. Ann taught me so much about the world right in front of me.

Another way I began to expand my personal horizons was through the world of online dating. Of course, many people had their horror stories, but being a single mother, I was extra cautious. My experiences ranged from lackluster to pleasant. I met a few professional men with fascinating and different lifestyles. It was nice to get a break and meet one guy for dinner, another for coffee, whatever, and just have stimulating adult conversation. My favorite experience was meeting an attractive, tall, blonde, Abercrombie photographer named Richard. I was elated when I met him, but in the end, he was too shy for my liking. I was never desperate in that I wanted to force something to work. I knew that if I were to become involved again, it had to feel totally right, for me and Sofia. I found myself always struggling with "when was the right moment" to tell a man that I had a child.

In the meantime, my baby girl was growing. We were bonding more and more with each day. One of my favorite memories was watching her try chocolate cake for the first time at seven months old. She bathed herself in icing, thoroughly enjoying her own baby chocolate *nirvana*. I was a happy mother, happy to watch my child grow and explore the world.

After five months in my Medicaid caseworker role, I interviewed for a new position. I ended up becoming a manager of various government assistance programs, including Medicaid, food stamps, and cash assistance. I met with six to eight clients a day, on average: single mothers like myself, homeless people, ex-convicts and families living far below the poverty line. Every situation had its own challenges and I felt I was making a difference in so many peoples' lives. I gave compassion and hope to my clients. The job was rewarding and at the same time reminded me of how fortunate I was, despite everything I had endured. An added benefit was that I received a large bump in my pay: I went from twelve to eighteen dollars an hour. I could finally cut back on my hours at LaScala and have more time with Sofia.

Not long after I had gotten my promotion, my dad, Kevin, totally surprised me. I was desperately needing a new car, as my old Toyota Camry had over two hundred thousand miles on it and wasn't long for this world. My father offered to go car shopping with me. As we strolled around the car lot, he asked me, out of all the cars we saw, which one did I really want? I pointed out an atomic blue Honda Civic, but added that I really couldn't afford a brand-new car and was preparing to buy a used car.

"Let's go take it for a test drive anyway," he said.

We found the salesman and took it for a drive around the neighborhood. When we returned, my dad told the salesman that he had worked for Honda for twenty-five years. In another breath, I heard him tell the rep that we would take the car! I could not believe my ears. My father looked at me and asked me how much I thought I could pay him a month. I quoted a figure and he agreed. He was buying me and Sofia a new car! I had seen the car so many times on the road and had visualized myself driving it: now, it was a reality, thanks to my dad.

Things were going great for me and my little girl. Still, I was lonely and wanted someone in my life, someone worthy of me and my amazing child. I continued to date but was constantly disappointed. Sometimes I felt selfish, thinking that I should feel that Sofia was enough. I struggled at times with my own self-assurance. I had kept a journal for some time, and one day I wrote down some points to ponder:

1. All the good and bad things in our lives give us wings to fly.
2. History helps us deal with today. It's not who we are.
3. Possessions do not define us.
4. Opinions can be barriers to learning. Be a blank slate.
5. "If we don't have peace, it's because we don't belong to each other."
   –Mother Teresa
6. All people are beautiful.

I kept reminding myself to be patient, and I tried to be "in the moment" with Sofia as much as I could. I was clearly searching for something, but I was still a "blank slate" with much to learn and much to live.

Miami Vices

My dear friend Pamela continued to be the supportive gal pal she always had been. Over spring break of 2007, she took a trip to Miami and met some new friends who lived in the area. She came home with her Floridian tales of adventure and I was intrigued. In October, she was heading to Miami once more for a weekend jaunt and asked me if I wanted to go with her. I hadn't had a real vacation since the fateful trip to the Outer Banks with my parents, but I was uncertain about leaving my two-year-old. My parents readily agreed to keep Sofia while I was gone. Pamela and I booked our flights after she arranged that we would be staying with her friend, Andres.

We landed in Miami at one in the morning. Andres' friend Jose, a real estate agent with thick curly hair, tan skin and a thick Spanish accent, picked us up in his Lexus. He took us to meet Andres where he worked, at a restaurant/bar called Casa Tua. I was completely taken in by a classic Miami ambience: fashionably dressed couples seated on white sofas, Latin music, the sounds of bongo drums, and everyone dancing as they spoke Spanish. Pamela and I danced our heels off that night. It was utter Shangri-La for a midwestern girl like me: I tried a glass of wine from a $15,000.00 bottle, wore a Versace coat, and was asked to drive a French vintner to his hotel! Juan, another friend of Andres, and I gave the wine merchant a lift before we finished the evening at an afterhours place. I just remember all the Latino men saying that I was an "all-American girl".

I guess I appeared wholesome and perhaps a bit naïve to them which, to be realistic, was dead-on. I was having the time of my life nonetheless.

The next morning, Juan phoned and inquired if I would accompany him to dinner that evening. I quietly asked Pamela and Andres if they would come along and they agreed. In the meantime, Andres lived a block from the beach, so we gathered up our things and headed over. As we walked along, I admired the expensive cars as they drove along the palm-tree lined boulevard.

October in Miami is usually warm, but there was a cool breeze that day so Pamela and I were wrapped up in our towels like human tacos as we slept on the beach. When we awoke, we ate lunch at a beachfront restaurant before we headed to the home of Alejandro, another friend of Andres', for coffee—real Columbian coffee, shipped over directly by Alejandro's family. He ushered us to a gorgeous veranda covered in tropical plants where I was served the most incredible cup of coffee I had ever had. Soon, it was time to head back to Andres' place and get ready for the evening's festivities.

We went to a Peruvian restaurant to meet Juan, who was a wine rep for the vintner I had met the night before. When we arrived, Juan was seated at a table for ten. We had dinner with a group of people from all over the world: France, Panama, Chile, Argentina, Columbia. Of course, Pamela was from Ireland, so I was the only native-born American at the table that night. It turned out to be less of a date and more of a dinner party, which suited me fine. After dinner, we were invited to the home of the Argentinian couple.

The house was like nothing I had ever seen: a massive, Mediterranean-style home in a gated community with an ivy-covered courtyard, marble columns, and lavish furnishings. There were roughly six of us in the group, and I want to be honest here and say that Pamela, Andres and I were readily intimidated—even a bit scared—within a short time of our arrival. Various illegal drugs appeared. It was like a scene from the old TV series *Miami Vice*. I had to patiently bide my time until Andres and the others were ready to leave.

Because of our late nights, Pamela and Andres slept in. I, having been a single mom and used to waking up with Sofia, required a little less sleep. The next morning, while the others were still in bed, I headed for the beach, not wanting to waste my chance to soak up the Miami sun. When I got there, I phoned Andres' friend Alejandro and thanked him for having us over for coffee the day before. He offered to come and join me at the beach.

Alejandro brought along some music for entertainment—never want to be hanging out without those Latin rhythms in the background—and we relaxed in the sun. A short time later, some gray clouds rolled in and there was a light drizzle. Alejandro asked me if I had ever swum in the ocean in the rain. I told him that I hadn't, and so we spent the rest of the afternoon floating in the swells while the rain washed over us. It was the most relaxing experience I'd ever had at the time.

Later, I had to catch my flight as my whirlwind trip came to an end. My world was suddenly much larger, and I had learned a few things about myself. I also felt more confident. Later, when I would dance to Latin music in my kitchen with Sofia, I would recall the freedom I had experienced on that trip.

I also knew that I wanted to travel more—and the sooner the better.

An Italian Restaurant in Dublin, Ohio

I went on with my life as a single mother, at times fighting off feelings of loneliness but most of the time just grateful to have Sofia and the stability that I had managed to build for the two of us. Priority one was setting a good example for her, and I wanted her to have a view of the world based on love, trust, and consistency. I couldn't let just anyone into our lives who would not appreciate her or be part of the balance I had created.

One night, after a shift at LaScala, I had some free time and phoned Pamela to see if she wanted to meet up. She was otherwise occupied, so I went solo and wound up at a place called Bar Louie. I hung out with some people who were having a birthday celebration for a guy named Adam. Adam was Egyptian-Caucasian, a handsome guy who had been raised in Bahrain. He spoke four languages, owned his own home, played guitar and drove a BMW. By the end of the evening, I had given him my phone number.

He took me to a Brazilian steakhouse on our first date. We went out afterward for music and dancing. All the while, I was trying to broach the subject of my daughter. When we said goodbye later that evening, I told him about Sofia. He responded that a child was "something new" to him but that he really had "no opinion". *Ok…*

Suffice to say that his attitude changed after that. I saw him little, if at all, after that. I was disappointed, but the experience did nothing but steel my resolve that I wouldn't have a man who wouldn't accept my child. Of course, I wanted, craved companionship, but I somehow knew that I needed to be patient. There were moments, too, when I was reminded of how lucky I was: like the time that Sofia asked my grandmother if she would like some lip gloss so she could "be pretty like Mommy". I knew a man was never going to love me like that, in this world or any other.

#

The holidays rolled around once more. I picked up extra shifts at LaScala while I adopted the festive attitude of the season. The Christmas ambience at the restaurant, along with all the corporate parties and such, made the season joyous and exciting.

I also continued to hang out with my co-worker, Ann. We went to museums, explored different cultures and sampled various ethnic foods. I loved our intellectual discussions. She encouraged me to read and I read many works written by Middle Eastern women. I learned and grew so much with her friendship.

The winter wore on, and of course after the glow of the holidays, the gray funk of January and the harsh Midwestern winter cast its shadow. I fought off depression as I battled the elements, digging my car out of snow and ice in my driveway and paying high heat bills. I tried not to sweat the daily grind or show my stress in front of my daughter, but sometimes things just piled up and I wanted to cry. One day Sofia flushed her rubber ducky down the toilet and I nearly lost it. How was I going to pay a plumber?

My great-grandmother's health also began to fail at this time. She was ninety-two and had been a huge part of my life. I loved her stories about seeing her first car, her first television, and her stories of going to a one-room schoolhouse. When I was younger, I played Scrabble with her and got a kick out of weighing myself on her doctor's office-style scale. She made each member of the family a special quilt. When she eventually passed at age ninety-four, it was a painful goodbye, but I took a huge part of her with me in my heart.

I had not heard from John for two years, nor had I received any support. The state of Ohio decided to put its foot down and demanded that he pay support or be incarcerated. He phoned me from jail, begging for me to lie and say that I didn't want his money. I had heard that he had begun to deny that Sofia was even his, and that made me angry. He had also remarried and taken on another child. I told him that the day he signed over his paternal rights to Sofia was the day I would help him out. He continued to whine and prey upon my sympathies, but I was finished. He could stay in jail if he could not step up as a father.

I hoped that one day her father's absence would not cause her to feel disenfranchised or that she was lacking something. I wanted her to be confident that she was more than enough and put on this earth for a reason. Meanwhile, none of this helped to alleviate my winter blues, but I pressed on, focusing on Sofia and the way she was becoming her own person, little by little, with each passing day. We had so much fun on winter evenings after I picked her up from one of her grandparents' homes or daycare. I was living paycheck to paycheck, so taking her to Chuck E. Cheese every night wasn't an option. Instead, we entertained ourselves at home. We listened to music and danced around our modest little duplex. We played dress-up and dined on mac and cheese. At bedtime, we read books and giggled over Dr. Seuss characters. I tried to cherish those moments.

Finally, spring arrived and I turned twenty-eight in April. Not long afterward, Ann invited me to a Pakistani wedding in Detroit. She loaned me an Indian ensemble: sheer, flowing fabric in a delicate pink. The wedding was an exotic experience with wonderful food and dancing. I met people from Iraq and India as well as Pakistan. It was a memorable experience and I'll always be grateful to Ann for sharing it with me. The exotic weekend celebration only fueled my desire for more adventure.

A short time after my Detroit excursion, Pamela stopped by my place one evening. She wanted me to attend a birthday party with her—in Ireland.

A Green Girl in a Green Land

amela either thought I was a great traveling companion or she saw how after our Miami adventure I had caught the "travel bug"—or maybe both. Her Uncle Kevin had contacted her, inviting her to attend her cousin Leanne's eighteenth birthday party in Ireland. The Irish consider the age of eighteen a milestone birthday. It was all going to be a big surprise for Pamela's cousin.

When Pamela suggested I come along, I was ecstatic. She had told me stories of her upbringing and her country many times, and my curiosity was piqued. It was an opportunity that I couldn't pass up. I had to find a way to make it work. It was just after tax season, so I had my refund money in the bank. The big consideration was Sofia: could I get my parents to take her while I went off to Europe for six days? Baca was also an option. She and Sofia were close and spent every Tuesday together. I was fortunate to have a large extended family with lots of cousins. Sofia had adapted to different environments within the family as well as daycare, as so many children of working single parents do. I wasn't concerned about her having separation anxiety when it came to me. She loved spending time with all her doting grandparents. I was far more likely to miss her before she noticed I was gone.

I phoned my mother. When I mentioned the trip with Pamela, her response was her non-committal trademark: she'd have to "think about it". The following day at work, I told my friend Ann about Pamela's invitation. She told me the trip would be life-changing, and that I needed to find a way to make it happen. Her words were just the nudge I needed. Soon, I had worked out child-care among Sofia's various grandparents. I had the green light to go to the Emerald Isle with my best friend!

#

After counting the days and weeks, the day of our departure finally arrived. After mother-daughter manicures, I smothered Sofia in hugs and kisses before dropping her off at her paternal grandmother's. At 2pm, Pamela and Edel pulled into my driveway. I emerged from my house with my luggage and a smile so broad it hurt. Pamela and her mom were taken aback by the number of suitcases I had. I told them my parents had bought me the set of luggage and I thought I needed all of it for an international trip. I would later learn the practical side of travel.

Pam and I flew from Dayton to Atlanta, and after a quick layover we were on our way to Ireland.

"Try to sleep," Pamela said, "so that when we arrive in Ireland at eight in the morning, (3am EST) you can start the day fresh."

I took advantage of the comforts of an international flight—movies, blankets—and tried to get some sleep. After two movies, *27 Dresses* and *Juno*, I was landing in no time. As I looked out the window of the plane, I noted that the country was indeed a patchwork of every color of green imaginable.

Pamela's Aunt Rita, a pleasant woman who was a bit of a spiritualist, was at the airport to greet us. I had met her before when she had come to visit Pam's family in Ohio. She greeted us warmly and we made our way through what I describe as a sing-song of lilting, Celtic accents. After maneuvering all my luggage, our adventures in Dublin ensued.

We motored along on that sunny May morning in Rita's small, blue SUV as I gazed wide-eyed at the countryside—well, after I adjusted as best I could to driving on the opposite side of the road! We zipped around roundabouts and along narrow roads lined with ancient stone walls. Houses and buildings looked smaller—and much older. I took photos of road signs that read *Baile Atha Cliath* (Dublin) and *Baile Munna* (Ballymun). I rolled down the window, taking in the fresh, crisp air that blew across the green hills. We were headed for a rendezvous point with Uncle Kevin, Leanne's father, but Rita could have taken me anywhere. I wanted to see it all!

We walked into the Carlton Hotel and found Pamela's uncle, a balding, jovial Irishman with warm brown eyes, seated at a table waiting for us. He greeted us with open arms. We all sat down and had tea and I listened to Pamela converse with her family. They even pronounced her name differently. I was beyond charmed.

Rita then drove us to Pamela's Aunt Tina's, where we would stay for the duration of our trip. This was the same house where Pam had grown up. Pam's seventeen-year-old cousin Calvin, whom I had met on several occasions when he had traveled to Ohio, was also there to greet us. We unwound for a bit, conversing and getting re-acquainted until Pamela, ever the instigator, suggested that our jetlag could be alleviated with a few drinks. We had some rum, took a few random and hilarious selfies with Calvin, until Pamela decided it was time to get ready for an evening on the town. While she was otherwise occupied, Calvin walked me around the neighborhood. The schoolgirls in uniforms, the quaint houses, the landscape—everything was so new.

Around four that afternoon, Pamela, Calvin and I boarded a double-decker bus headed for Temple Bar, the cobble-stoned, shopping and nightclub district along the River Liffey. As we walked along the busy streets amid throngs of people, I was amazed at the plethora of accents: French, Italian, Spanish. There were people from all over the globe. We went to various pubs, drank, danced, sang and met all sorts of fascinating people. At four in the morning, we had to call it quits. Calvin had school later that day and I was exhausted, the drinks merely having postponed the jetlag that hit me like a ton of bricks. Pamela was still on fire, with no end to her energy in sight. Tina had been calling, checking to make sure the kids were not dead in the proverbial "ditch". Finally, Pamela gave in and we called a taxi.

I slept until one the following afternoon. After a breakfast of oatmeal, I went for a run at a nearby park. A little exercise and fresh air did wonders—I was ready for the next phase of our adventure: Leanne's birthday party.

Glass in her Foot,
and a Trip to the Chipper

On my second evening in Ireland, Rita drove Pamela and me to Uncle Kevin's house. When we arrived, Rita opened the gate and we pulled into the neighbor's driveway or "car park" as the Irish call it. The property was a rental that Kevin owned, and Rita informed us that it was currently leased to some Italian engineers.

A man was in the carpark, loading a van. He dropped what he was doing and walked over to greet us. His head was shaved, and he wore a white shirt and dress pants. It was hard with his shaved head to determine his age, but to me he seemed older. He introduced himself in an Italian accent as Carlo and, after shaking all our hands, helped Rita with her bag. After helping us inside, he soon disappeared.

At around seven o'clock, after all the party guests had arrived, a limo came to take us out on the town of Dublin. The city was so lovely, with all its parks, gardens, and old buildings. We arrived at La Peniche, a restaurant located on a barge on a canal, where we had amazing food as we celebrated Leanne's birthday. When her cake was brought to the table, everyone in the restaurant sang "Happy Birthday" to her. After dinner, we were entertained with guitar music as we laughed and drank the night away. When the celebration was over, the limo took us back to Tina's place.

The next day, we were off to Stephen's Green, a gorgeous park in the Dublin City Centre. The park was full of people walking around, feeding the swans, lounging on park benches. Children played all about. It was a beautiful sight.

Next, we ventured over to historic Grafton Street with its buildings that housed iconic Irish businesses such as Brown Thomas, Weir and Sons, and Bewley's Grafton Street Café. Grafton Street was a circus-like atmosphere with all manner of street performers: mimes, musicians and other artists all "busking" for money. We ate lunch at Burdocks, the oldest "chipper" in Ireland, indulging in some traditional fish and chips. With our brown bags full of greasy goodness, we walked to Temple Bar and sat on some steps to eat our lunch. As I sat there eating, I observed the people going by and noted that some of their accents were thick brogues that I couldn't make out. I looked over at Pamela after noting one passer-by: "Did you understand that guy?" I asked. "No," she replied. I was relieved.

After lunch, we headed back to Tina's. It was time for another night of celebration: the night of Leanne's official birthday party. While Pamela took one of her lengthy showers, I decided to go for a run. When I returned, I began rummaging through my suitcase for something to wear. I had wanted to wear my red dress, a form-fitting, glamorous piece that I had purchased at Victoria's Secret, but something had spilled on it in my bag. When I went into the bathroom to take my shower, the water was freezing! I got out and said to Pamela: "I'll skip the shower. There's no hot water and I'd rather be dirty than take a cold shower." Pamela called for Tina to help.

Who knew that pushing the button labeled "Heat" would get you a hot shower? I felt so silly. Tina also got the stain out of my red dress, so I was able to wear it after all. Pamela wore black in contrast to my red. We were a couple of "statements" as usual.

Rita came to pick us up and we headed to Kevin's house once more. Leanne and seven of her friends were all seated around the table socializing when we walked in. We had some drinks and hung out for a bit before the limo arrived once more. After we took a few photos, we were off to the Russell Court Hotel for Leanne's big night.

As we rode along, a young girl seated next to me, about twenty-one or so, kept changing the music and shouting out the window. Pamela and I, though not much older, exchanged looks of derision. We toured the city for about an hour until we arrived at the hotel, where Rita, Kevin and his girlfriend Polly, along with Adam (Pamela's other cousin) were there to meet us.

The evening was fun, with lots of wine, food, and socializing. I noticed that Carlo, the Italian engineer, was also in attendance. He approached me and we started talking. We were both "strangers in a strange land", so it was nice to have someone to talk to about the whole Irish experience. I was surprised to find out he wasn't much older than I.

Carlo told me he was from the island of Sardinia. He had moved to Ireland to do an internship when he was twenty-four and he had never left. I told him that this was my first international trip and shared with him some of my experiences thus far. As our conversation went on, he eventually inquired if I had a significant other, and I told him "No."

"Why are you still single?" he asked.

"Because I have not found the person who adds amazing happiness to my life, yet," I responded.

There was a nightclub next door to the reception room where the party was held, and Pamela and I, along with Carlo and several others, spent the evening going back and forth, drinking and dancing. Pamela and I danced with some boys who were really good dancers— "raver"-types. Pamela kicked off her shoes to dance, and later, when she went to get them, they had disappeared. "Who steals shoes?" she asked. We went searching everywhere but had no luck. Pamela was forced to go barefoot the rest of the evening. Things only got worse when later in the evening she stepped on a piece of broken glass and cut her foot. At one point, she was riding piggy-back on someone as she searched for her shoes.

Things were getting crazy. We told various people of our dilemma and Carlo came to the rescue, offering us a lift home in his Italian car.

As we rode along, we passed a chipper and I asked Carlo if we could stop and get something to eat. All that dancing had worked up an appetite! Shoeless Pamela waited in the car while Carlo and I went into the chipper. I was amused when I realized that the people working in the chipper were Italian as well. Carlo bought me some fish and chips to go and we were off again. I shared my food with Carlo, feeding him as we drove along.

The next morning, Pamela was struggling to remove the glass from her foot. With a little help from Tina, she finally prevailed. We took the morning slowly, having expended our energy the night before. Later, Pamela took me to see Bray Head Mountain. We took the bus to Dublin city center where we would catch the train to Bray. We ran into an Italian girl we had met on our first night in Dublin. We chatted a bit before catching our train. When we got to Bray, Pamela and I headed for a coffee shop.

"Let's get a shot of espresso so that we have energy to climb the mountain," she suggested.

I agreed, but after a shot each, I wasn't feeling much more energetic and neither was Pamela. We ended up drinking four shots each! As we were walking out of the café, a group of four Irish guys were walking in. They asked us what we were up to, and we told them we were about to climb the mountain. We ended up sitting down with them and I don't remember ever laughing so hard. Of course, Pamela and I were flying high on caffeine!

We set out on our hike up the mountain. Bray is a city on the Irish Sea, so as you climb up the mountain, the sea gets farther and farther away beneath you. We zipped up the mountain in thirty-five minutes. The espresso was working! The climb was beautiful with all the wildflowers and various trees. At the top, there was a cross, and we could look out and see for miles over land and water.

Of course, after hanging out on the mountaintop, our energy waned and it took us an hour to make the hike back down. When we arrived back at the train station, we bumped into the Irish guys and they asked us to get together later that night. Some other friends also wanted to meet up with us, but Pamela and I were beat. We decided to meet up with Kevin for a quiet dinner. We met Kevin and Adam for some Chinese food and then went back to Tina's and turned in for the night.

I was slowly falling in love with Pamela's native land: especially the language. Whenever I heard words like "lads" and "luv" I was enamored. I learned that a vacation was a "holiday" and that "locked out" meant "drunk". Pamela and I both agreed we would love to move to Ireland in the future. Of course, we were two young and beautiful girls in the middle of a birthday celebration and enjoying all the nightlife of Temple Bar. Why wouldn't we have wanted to move there? It would have been easy enough for Pamela to move there, as she was already a citizen, but I was an American single mom with a child to support. I considered my Irish flights of fancy to be just that.

#

The last day of the trip happened to be Pamela's twenty-seventh birthday. We had an easy morning before going to the grocery to buy some things for me to take back to the States. I purchased chocolates, sweets, and other items for Sofia. Pamela's uncle decided to give us a countryside car tour. I rode in the backseat of the black BMW, gazing out at rolling green pastures and prehistoric forts. The Dublin hills were covered in every color of green one could imagine!

We had takeaway (take-out) pizza for dinner with Tina's family. We all sang "Happy Birthday" to Pam and then Tina took us to the Four Seasons Ice Bar. Pam had heard that Colin Farrell had been spotted there from time to time. We had a martini with Tina and then she dropped us at Temple Bar.

By this time, Pamela and I were both broke and decided we'd have to wing it. It wouldn't be the first time that a couple of pretty young girls managed a free drink or two. We stopped at Foggy Dew's where things were rather low key, although the evening was still young. When we hopped over to Fitzsimons, the night finally kicked off.

Pamela and I began chatting with two guys who had just finished playing their gig and were putting away their guitars. They were brothers, James and Frank. After speaking with them for a bit, I went off to "check out the place" while Pamela hung out with the brothers. Fitzsimons is three stories and there was a huge crowd. I met loads of "lads and lasses" and proceeded to get "locked out" and have a great time—trying to forget that Rita was picking me up bright and early at 8am the next morning. At one point in the evening, Pamela suggested that we go back to Frank's and James' place. We had no taxi money, and I said, "Why not?" (What was I thinking?) It was my last night in Ireland, and I guess I was going "all in".

We rode in Frank's and James' van out to their house in County Meath. It was an hour outside of Dublin and in retrospect I don't recommend anyone try this. Pamela and I had a great time with the brothers, however, who ended up picking up their guitars and serenading us! It was a fun evening and at six in the morning the brothers paid the fifty euros for our cab fare and we were back at Tina's house by seven.

I arrived at the airport, exhausted and hungover, only to find out my flight had a six-hour delay. I grabbed some food with the airline voucher and then settled into a chair for a nap. When I awoke, I had two hours to go before my flight, so I began to write in my journal about my incredible holiday, as the Irish would say.

"What are you doing?" a male voice asked me in an Irish brogue.

I looked up to see a dark, ruggedly handsome face.

"I just had the most amazing six days of my life," I said, "and I need to write everything in my journal because I don't want to miss a thing."

He introduced himself as Paul and sat down next to me. We had a great conversation until it was time to board.

Paul was on my flight as well, and he carried my bags on board and lifted them into the overhead compartment for me. I sat down and then an elderly lady sat down next to me. I wasn't feeling well at all and needed to stretch out. I spied some empty seats in a middle row at the rear of the plane, near where Paul was sitting. I got up and walked back to the row of seats. As I stretched out, I commented to Paul that I needed a good nap. I asked him if he would wake me when the food was coming, and he kindly assented. A couple of hours later, I felt a gentle nudge.

"The food is coming," Paul said.

He eventually moved to a seat next to me and we talked the whole flight. Paul was a rugby player on his way to the States for the first time. When we landed in Atlanta, we parted ways. I wished him the best first experience in America.

Because of my delay, I missed my connecting flight and had to stay in a hotel that evening. I had the best night of sleep I'd had in over a week. The next morning, I flew home to Dayton.

The first thing I did was go and pick up my daughter. I was so excited to see her. I was so happy to hold her and give her the presents I had bought. The next few days, I felt like I was in a dream state. Of course, much of it was jet lag, but I was forever changed. I was home, but everything felt different: in a good way. I remember driving to work that first day back, blasting Leona Lewis's "Bleeding Love" on the radio, feeling on top of the world.

An Italian in my Inbox

I was at my desk my first day back to work, my mind still reeling from my Ireland escape. After sharing details of my trip with my co-workers, I sat down to check my email to see if Pamela had written. I had left her back in Ireland with her family and it had been two days since we had spoken. When I opened my inbox, I was surprised to see an email from Carlo, the Italian engineer, in his charming take on English:

Sent: Thursday, May 22, 2008
Subject: A thought for you from Italy
Hi Laurie

This is Carlo, your new Italian-Irish friend!

Welcome back at home!

Are you happy to be back or you wanted to stay more in Ireland? I am sure you enjoyed the place.

I would be glad to receive some pics from you, just to remember the party we had together. It was great and I remember with a nice smile something from you that night.

It has been so funny to meet you and I'd like to see you again, doesn't matter when or where!

Kisses from Sardinia...

Regards, C

Carlo had also given me an address to IM him. To say the least, I was surprised. I tried to remember exactly when I had given Carlo my email address. I mean, it was a party after all, and I was certainly doing my fair share of celebrating Pam's cousin's eighteenth birthday! After thinking that I must have given it to him the night of the party at the hotel, I re-read the email and decided Carlo was simply wanting pictures from the evening. I responded the next day:

Sent: Friday, May 23, 2008
Subject: A thought for you from Italy
Hello Carlo,

I am back home, and it feels like I may need a week or so to re-adjust to life, work, and so on. It was wonderful meeting you and getting to hang out - good times! I loved Ireland in all aspects - it was beautiful, and my holiday was extremely exciting with lots of things going on. I am unable to send you pictures right now b/c I am at work, but when I get my pictures uploaded I will be sure to send them to you. It would be great to see you again also. You are always welcome in OHIO.... Great hearing from you.

Take care.. Laurie

I emailed Pam, who was still in Ireland. I told myself I wanted to catch up with her and give her the update on my return home—but my mind was all over the place. I forwarded her the curious email from our Italian friend:

Sent: Friday, May 23, 2008
Subject: FW A thought for you from Italy
[To: Pamela]
Pamela - I need your phone number. *The letter below is from Carlo (so sweet) just wanted to let you read it.* It is quite crazy to be at work right now. I am on some sort of high energy buzz and nothing

really seems normal. On the way to work I was blasting the radio (weird driving after so long) - and I slept yesterday from 3 until this morning at 6 - I guess I was a bit tired. It was around 75 degrees and sunny yesterday so that was nice. My mind is everywhere and spinning in circles after all the crazy times. Sofia was so happy to see me - we had good times together. I have a 3-day weekend starting tomorrow so that will help some to ease back to this life in Dayton. Sorry I missed your call (sleeping)! I hope you have lovely, amazing experiences for the rest of your time in Ireland. I wish I could be there. What a whirlwind of experiences...... Well I guess I am going to start working (at least pretend or try????) I will send you all the pictures tonight. I did a slide show to watch all the pictures from beginning to end - it was so funny to see the entire week documented in 500 pictures and 4 movies.... Thank you so much for the best experiences ever!!! The next chapter has begun, and our lives are changed forever!!! Love your Bestest Friend...... Laurie

When I received Pam's somewhat cryptic reply, I was taken aback. Pam was never one to project thoughts on men when it came to our friendship. She was rather protective of me, given all that she had witnessed in my former marriage.

Sent: Saturday, May 24, 2008
Subject: FW A thought for you from Italy
[From: Pamela]
Laurie,
I hope all is perfect and well with you. What's going on? I hope you have settled in nicely, but not to much because we have a whole world and a whole life to live out there. The trip was amazing and to experience it with you was even better. It honestly was the time of my life. I don't feel that coming back to Dayton is a reality at this point. I love this, I really appreciate everything about these

moments, so many encounters and laughs.... Carlo's message to you is really sweet, he is just one of those genuine lovely guys. He really likes you, I think everyone knows. Leanne says he wants everyone to get together for dinner when he returns. I bet he will ask about coming to America so he can see you. Awe, is it love??? James and Frank want to come over too.... I am so sad that you are not here.

Much love hippie friend –

Interesting. I thought back to my first impressions of Carlo. He was ever the gentleman, his demeanor rather austere compared to the rest of us party animals. I thought of our conversation at the hotel, and of the trip to the Dublin chipper in the middle of the night. I shook my head and focused on having a relaxing Memorial Day weekend with Sofia. On Sunday, I emailed Carlo several photos with a short polite note. I received a nearly instantaneous reply:

Sent: Sunday, May 25, 2008
Subject: 22 Pictures for You
Laurie,
Great pictures! Thanks
If you see around that beautiful girl shown in most of the pictures with me....please say to her that she was amazing! :-)
I'm going to change my personal life from tomorrow, as soon as I'll be back in Dublin. In fact, meeting you I realized something, something I didn't speak with you about...
Thanks to you I realized I'm not happy with my actual girlfriend and I think would be the best finish this story. Probably I needed to meet someone from Ohio to understand it...
Thanks Laurie, you made my way brighter....

Wow.

There was nothing "lost in translation" there. I didn't know what to think. Certainly, I'd never had a man open up to me in such an abrupt fashion, ESL issues notwithstanding. I was charmed, curious, and maybe even a little intimidated. I wondered what sort of conversations Pamela was having with her family about Carlo back in Ireland as I wrote my reply:

Sent: Tuesday, May 27, 2008
Subject: 22 Pictures for You
Hey Carlo-
How are you? I am back at work - living my life in Ohio! The weather has been nice since I have been home; although, I miss Ireland and Pamela a ton. The trip was amazing in all aspects. Ireland is beautiful, meeting awesome people, and having total freedom to do whatever / whenever says it all. I am having a hard time adjusting back to an 8-5 job and all that goes with that. I am ready for another holiday already..... A question that I am wondering? Why after meeting me did you then realize that you were not happy with your current girlfriend?? Just curious?? Well, I hope you have a lovely week and I will start planning my next holiday (b/c I am so so ready to have a relaxing holiday after my fun filled week in Ireland). Take care, Laurie

I was of course the proverbial Juliet on the balcony, prodding Romeo for more words of ardent supplication, whether I was aware of it or not. This whole thing was such a shock, however. It wasn't long before I had some answers to my questions:

Sent: Tuesday, May 27, 2008
Subject: 22 Pictures for You

Hi Laurie,

It's good hearing from you and I am happy to know that you're planning already the next holiday....live the life at its best!

Sometimes life is strange and it gives us signals we have to understand.

I was dating 10 months with a lovely girl, older 4 years than me. I made her happy and I gave to her everything she wanted...and I thought I was happy.

But then I met a girl from Ohio... and she has been for me like a bolt from the blue.

After that night I thought that probably I was not happy as I could be.

If someone can cross my life with these results, make me forgetting who is my current girlfriend, probably this girlfriend is not the woman of my life.

I spent all the following Sunday with these thoughts in my mind, and I didn't want to meet you that day because of this reason, not because I was busy as I texted to Pam...

It's not simple to carry out these thoughts from my heart, especially because I am writing in another language and to an almost stranger...

Now I'm suffering, from her, because she is destroyed and for myself, because I feel alone, far from home and from the people who love me, but I am sure I made the right decision.

The life must be lived at 100% or more, not at 50%... Can you realize that you came in Ireland to change my life?! Life is incredible…

All the Best dear Laurie.

Take care, C.

All I could do was think about the guy in the driveway who greeted us when we arrived at Uncle Kevin's, the guy who had stayed in the background while Pam and I danced the night away with young Irishmen, the guy who had seen two crazy young inebriated girls safely home in the middle of the night....*Was this for real?*

When I wrote him back, I chose my words carefully.

Sent: Wednesday, May 28, 2008
Subject: 22 Pictures for You

Hello again Carlo...

Life is crazy - understanding what we want vs. where we are at in life. How to get where we want to be vs. enjoying the now which is all we really have. You can plan for the future, but in reality you have to make the best of what we are experiencing at each moment. I think we have similar views on life (positive outlook)! It is refreshing to meet someone that has the ability to understand what living is about. Thank you for sharing with me in regards to your life. I hope the best for you - whatever is to come in your future. It is a crazy thing when life presents you with situations that make you evaluate, grow, and learn about yourself. The trip to Ireland has also changed me in many ways - as I feel that I am still on a holiday. I have been very relaxed and just wanting to enjoy what the day brings. Routines are created when you are doing the same things day in and day out - once outside and away from the normal routine - this has given me a new way to view my life and in its current standing. I appreciate all experiences, but the trip to Ireland has opened my eyes to a whole new, huge world. I think at this age -28- evaluating, understanding, and knowing where we want our lives to be is huge. Decisions we make each day lead to where our future will take us. All in all while remembering that all we have is the NOW. Great talking with you - my Italian-Irish friend!

Ciao, Laurie

A short time later, Carlo wrote back:

Sent: Wednesday, May 28, 2008
Subject: 22 Pictures for You

Laurie,

Since I received your email, I probably read it 10 times... (as they say here: fock!)

It has been the only thing that made me smile and feeling comfortable since yesterday :-)

I really appreciate your point of view about life, especially life related to our age and it's great hearing from you what you think about it.

We have very similar views of the same thing.

It sounds very, very strange, but meeting you has been for me a new chapter of my life.

Thanks for your deep thoughts and for sharing them with me.

A particular sentence of your email will be written for ever in my mind:

"Decisions we make each day lead us to where our future will take us"

Thanks Laurie.

I think I met an extraordinary person...and I would love to stay in contact with you.

Take care and Ciao, C.

His message took my breath away. My mind went in a million directions as I pondered being wooed by an Italian man I barely knew— in cyberspace, no less. I felt comfortable enough, given his connection to Pam's family, along with the fact that I had met him, albeit briefly. Eventually my thoughts rolled around to reality: I was a single mother. If I were going to pursue this romance, electronic or not, Sofia was part of the package. I thought long and hard, deleting and re-typing several times, until I sent my next message:

Sent: Wednesday, May 28, 2008
Subject: 22 Pictures for You

Hello Carlo...

I have enjoyed your emails and would like to find out a bit more about you... Questions?? So, where did you grow up, family, college, hobbies, and anything else you may like to share with your new friend from Ohio. I would like to share some things with you as well. I grew up in a small town in Ohio called North Lewisburg. One stop light small to be exact. While in high school I played basketball and softball. I decided to go to college at Wright State University and play on the softball team. Ok, so I know that when we briefly spoke about our lives I told you that I just haven't found the person whom I am choosing to spend the rest of my life with yet. And I haven't: It is a long story and I did not feel that when first meeting someone it is appropriate to share such personal things. Now that I am getting to know you a little I would like you to really know me and a bit of what I have went through to make me who I am today. All just experiences - so then when I was 19 I met a guy who joined the army and I thought that I found someone that I would like to spend the rest of my life with: we were married when I was 21. Married for 4 years - it turned out that he was not at all the right person for me in all aspects. He did not treat me with respect, nor did we have the type of connection I am looking for - at age 25 I had a daughter, Sofia who is now 3 years old. When Sofia was born my now x-husband left and started a new life while I started a new life with my daughter. For the past 3 years it has been my daughter and I living in a house together. She has totally helped me become who I am today. I have gained so much strength, patience, and maturity after she has come along. You already know that I am a person who thinks that things happen for a reason - my daughter has added to my life immensely. My x-husband is not involved with my daughter by his choice. Although, his family is very close with

Sofia and I. That is a very brief overview of my past that I would like share. I feel that after going through what I have experienced I am a much wiser and stronger person. I think things in life build upon one another and get us to where we need to go next. Difficult times in life build character and show us what we are capable of doing. I would not change anything in my past for I wouldn't be where I am at today without it. I enjoy writing with you across the ocean - it is crazy how some people come into your life at a certain time and add something new, different, interesting.... So, I would love to hear more about you and how you have made it to where you are today. Bye for now, Laurie

I braced myself for a "Nice knowing you, see you around Temple Bar sometime, maybe". I felt vulnerable as I waited impatiently for his reply. When it came, I couldn't have been more overwhelmed:

Sent: Thursday, May 29, 2008
Subject: 22 Pictures for You
Dear Laurie,
It is simply amazing.
I met an extraordinary girl that Saturday and this is something I am thinking about every time I know something more from you.
I don't know what, but that night, I saw something in your eyes which attracted me a lot, as I wrote to you, and only now, day after day, I am understanding why. Life sometimes is not easy, and only the best persons can learn from it. I'm so glad to hearing something very personal about you and Sofia...and if you're pleased, I'd really like to have a picture of Sofia and you together.
For sure, your past experiences made you as you are now and the life gave you the best present a young woman can have, a daughter. I would like to share with you something of my life as well.

I grew up in a small town in the south part of Sardinia, where I lived with my parents and my sister (2 years younger than me). When I was 18 I decided to go to the University in the main city of our island, Cagliari, to try to get an engineering degree. This was bigger than a challenge for me, as in Italy is not simple to get a degree especially in engineering. But I was more than determined, because I wanted to change my life in better and have something my parents never could give me. With some efforts, between basketball games and gym workouts, at the age of 24 I graduated as an engineer...and I thought the life was starting to smile at me. Few months before the degree I met a beautiful girl and we felt in love. It was June '04, and I started to search for a job, but nothing good was happening. The Italian economy was not doing very well, so it was not easy to find a job as an engineer. All my relatives and friends and my girlfriend were very close to me, but I started to be not happy about the situation. Suddenly, in September '04, I received a phone call from an Italian Company which I contacted few days before. They were looking for someone able to draw technical drawings for a project in Ireland...They met me, I liked them as they liked me, and with no doubts, after only 4 days I arrived in Ireland...At that moment I chose my personal life vs my family and my girlfriend, and this was the beginning of the problems for the next 4 years. I was very happy with that girl and I loved her a ton, but she was coming from a rich family and she was not able to understand my efforts in a strange country. As my skills and the desire to have a nice career were growing, my girlfriend was sad and she was getting sick for my absence. For this reason, after 4 years, hundreds of flights to stay close to her and a house built together, she forced me to take a decision: my career or her.

I think these are decisions can change your life and as a friend of mine told me once... "decisions we make each day lead where to our future will take us"...

I'm pushing very hard with my job, as I told you I left the position as a simple employee to become co-owner of the Company who took me as an apprentice only 4 years ago, and I'm doing all of this for myself and for the woman whom I'll share my life with.

I never wrote any letter in English long as this one...and this is dedicated to you, to make you knowing me better and to share with you something very personal of my life.

That's incredible as an Ocean sometimes can be really nothing!

Talk to you soon Dear Laurie.

Ciao, C.

Life gave you the best present a young woman can have, a daughter...An ocean can sometimes be really nothing....

Was this really happening? I read Carlo's email at least ten times, utterly astonished with his words. I shared it with Pamela and even my Aunt Lynn, who was skeptical, of course. What did I really know about this strange Italian, after all? It didn't matter. I couldn't wait for the next email.

Sent: Thursday, May 29, 2008
Subject: 22 Pictures for You

Carlo,

I am really impressed with you writing in a second language. I could not imagine - I took 8 Spanish classes in high school/college combined. There is really no way I could write in a second language like you have been. Did you know any English prior to your move to Ireland? Was that a difficult transition from one culture, people, surrounds to a completely new everything? Ireland was my first experience out of America and it has been such an eye opener for me. I am still in awe of what that trip was... No words can truly describe it. Since I have been home I have just been enjoying my life more than ever. I feel as if I am still on a holiday. After work just hanging out with Sofia - last night Sofia and I went and bought $120 worth of flowers to plant in flower baskets. That was a new experience as well. I got to walk through so many flowers and choose colors, textures, vines, etc... and then come home and planted them. It was so relaxing and a beautiful finished product. My next holiday is in 29 days - I am going to the beach in North Carolina (Emerald Isle is the name of the island) to just kick back, lay at the beach, and spend time with my family. 10 people (my mom, dad, Sofia, my aunt, cousin, great aunt and uncle, and grandpa / grandma all rented a house on the beach and we are just going to enjoy 7 days of good times....

Sofia just turned 3 last Saturday - we have been celebrating every day since. Her party is next Sunday so I figure she should just celebrate until then. Just little things like going to a carnival, having a friend spend the night, going to a block party, having ice cream and cookies at McDonald's, choc'cake w/ a candle (I bought it in Ireland), and tonight she got a card in the mail (and as she said "I got some bucks"). Our grandma gave her $20 with the card. It has been fun just hanging out and enjoying each day. The weather has been sunny and warm which is a plus.

Lovely writing with you. I have really enjoyed getting to know more about you. As well as, getting to share things from my life with you. So more questions for you: What does a day in the life of Carlo consist of (start to finish)? How many other Italians are in Ireland with you working? How often do you travel home? Have you ever traveled to America? What do your parents do?

I look forward to hearing from you,

Take care and enjoy,

Laurie

Sent: Friday, May 30, 2008
Subject: 22 Pictures for You

Laurie,

Thanks very much for the compliments with regards to English as a second language for me!

I've improved it a lot during the last few years, although I took 3 classes in high school. Once arrived here, it improved day after day by itself! Still a long way must be done, and it's my intention improve it through some TOEFL course as I'm planning to do very soon. This could be of two meanings; first of all I'll improve it and second, I'd need a kind of certificate to try to get my next challenge...an MBA here in Ireland! I know, it could sound strange, but I think that we never know what is behind the corner. If I'll spend all my career in my Company, probably I'll not need it, but... who knows?! In case I pursue it, I'll have to spend every weekend for 2 years following classes and exams, but at the end, it could be another big personal achievement.

Any time you mention some place in your emails, I open the Google Earth window in my pc just to understand you a little better...I saw North Lewisburg, Wright State University, Dayton and the Emerald Isle. It's great to see something of any place you speak about! I always dreamed about to go in the States, but I never had the chance. Can I tell you something? Sofia is really cute! While working here in my office, few times during the day I looked the pictures...they made me smiling. She has a smart and clever look....and I think you're doing the best with and for her. My compliments Laurie! It's great that you spend a lot of time with her, she really needs you and she can learn a lot from you. Anyway...give to her my best wishes for her 3rd birthday!

Since I arrived here in Ireland, challenges started in my life. A new language, a brand new career in front of me, a strange City in a strange Country, different people, habits, culture and places...what an amazing Adventure! I think all these things worked to make me what I am now. This experience is making me different a lot from my old friends which decided to stay in Italy. In the beginning it was not simple, but as you already know, now this place is becoming to be my second home, although I feel like I'll not stay here for the rest of my life.

Actually, in our Company here in Ireland we have three Italian guys working with me, while I think in all Ireland, the Italians could be around 10 thousands (most of them, about 90% are involved in some restaurant's businesses).

My work position permits me to travel very frequently to Italy. I usually go in Sardinia few days every month. I can take two flights, going through Milan or Rome, otherwise a direct connection with a low coast company (but I really prefer take two comfortable flights rather than a single cheap one!).

Usually my days are very similar one to each other. I get up at 6:30 and arrive in the office at 7:30. Once there, I manage the teams, emails, contacts, banks, invoices, meetings, accountants, bla bla bla, bla bla bla! In the evening I leave the work at 8 and I go straight to the gym, where I meet the friends who I train with. Then I come back at home only at 10:30 or later, just to have a nice shower and a fast dinner...

What else...ah, sure, the last question!

My mother spent all her life to make my sister and I what we are now, while my father retired one year ago from the Italian Air Force. Now they're close to my sister who is finishing her study in law and their bigger efforts are dedicated to the new house they're just buying in a beautiful sea place in Sardinia. (Follow the link I've attached to this email and let me know if you see the house. If you see it, just take a look at the amazing places surrounding it!).

Tomorrow morning I'll take the car to head to Belfast, the English capital of the English part of Ireland. I'll buy some IKEA furniture for the office, we just renovated it!

What about you? I'm really enjoying to know you and your life better and share with you something about my life…and when I start my day reading your email…everything goes well!

At this time I think Pam is already with you. As soon as you see her just give her my goodbye! I didn't have the chance to meet her since I came back in Dublin.

Dear Laurie, time to say bye, just for now.

Pam had indeed arrived home and I could not wait to get together with my dearest friend—who had recently landed back in Ohio. So much had transpired during our time apart. Our first get-together was at a park with Sofia and Hayley, Pamela's younger sister.

Sent: Saturday, May 30, 2008
Subject: 22 Pictures for You

Carlo,

Pamela made it home safe. We hung out this evening along with Sofia and Hayley (Pamela has a younger sister who is 7 named Hayley). Sofia and Hayley are friends which makes for an all around good time. It was so nice finally getting to speak with Pamela about our experiences. It was like going through all new experiences with someone for 7 days and then having to return to a completely different world where no one can completely relate to what you just experienced. I would show people pictures, tell stories - people thought it sounded cool, but they could not feel what I was feeling. So good to have Pamela home - we hung out for the evening. It was nice hearing about the rest of her trip and discussing all the amazing times. I don't know if I told you about my friendship with Pamela. Pamela and I have been best friends since we were 19 (Pamela) and 20 (myself). We have gone through so many things together, completely get each other, and have amazing times together no matter what the occasion. So, to get to experience a whole new world (for me) with my best friend - WOW is all I can say. Pamela would love to move to Ireland after the experience. Pamela and I both feel that life should be lived without regrets. Don't look back and say I wish I would have. We had the opportunity to visit Ireland when we first met. Nothing in the way of spending an entire summer in Ireland. We had no idea the value of that - we chose to spend the summer in Ohio. It was a great summer with lots of memories, but Ireland would have been amazing. All in time - things happen for reasons! I do feel that at 28 I was able to value my experiences so much more than I ever could have at the age of 20. Growing up is just crazy - one day you are picking a college and living that life, and the next you are working and all grown up. The now is all we have.

The past is gone, the future uncertain, so stay in the moment!

So, every Saturday I work at my second job which is a server at a Fine Dining Restaurant named "LaScala Italian Ristorante" in Dublin, OH. That is kind of crazy. The owners are two brothers who grew up in Ohio; although, there father immigrated here from Italy when he was 25 or so…. I have to drive 1 hour from my house in order to work each Saturday. Saturday mornings are usually spent around my house just hanging out with Sofia, having breakfast, and getting ready for the day. On the weekdays Sofia and I have to be out the door by 7am and I start work at 7:30am. Sofia goes to preschool while I am at work. When I get to work I interview welfare clients in order for them to get government assistance. It is a crazy job, but I enjoy it. Dealing with people at their hardest times makes me appreciate what I have so much. At lunch I eat with my friend Ann most days. She was raised in India until she went to college. Our 1 hour lunch break is spent at art museums, shopping, coffee shops, and other places. I like to make the most of my time. She is an awesome person that I met at my job. After work I usually run a couple miles, pick up Sofia, go to the bank, cook dinner, hang out, sometimes yoga, read - and the day is over. Sunday's are my only day I have off so I try to catch up on things, take is easy, and spend time with Sofia. Pamela and I live about 5 minutes from one another so we get to see each other all the time. Well, I think I just wrote a novel. I find it really easy to write with you while sharing what my life is. Hope you have a lovely day today Carlo! Bestest, Laurie

Sent: Sunday, June 1, 2008
Subject: 22 Pictures for You

Laurie,

Today the Irish weather was amazing!

No clouds, no wind and an incredible sun...if tomorrow morning will be the same I'll face a good challenge...my first swim into the Ocean! I'll let you know.

I remember you already told me about your friendship with Pam when we briefly spoke about us. Friendship is one of the most important thing in life and it's great when you can share your experiences with some one else close to you, and able to understand how you feel like.

If I'm not wrong, tomorrow will be the great Sofia's party...I hope she'll enjoy it and all of you will have a great time.

Day after day I'm knowing you better and this sounds strange to me. It never happened something similar before and I really don't feel the distance. But, the most amazing thing is that you look like such an interesting person even with an ocean between us!

I'd like to know something more about you...

What kind of music do you like? You wrote to me that sometimes in the evening you read some books... Which kind of books? and then...what's your favourite perfume? Although I probably smelled it, I didn't recognize it.

I hope you'll enjoy your Sunday off and please drive safe in your way back from Dublin to Dayton after the work at the restaurant... Every time it's a pleasure hearing from you.
Talk to you soon, C.

My "favourite perfume"? What books did I like? I'd never had a man ask me about what I liked, or even care. This was so unlike any conversation I had ever had with anyone. I responded in kind, answering his questions. I also had a few of my own:

Sent: Sunday, June 1, 2008
Subject: 22 Pictures for You
Carlo,
...Currently on my ipod I have been listening to Leona Lewis. What about you, what type of music do you prefer? Do you or have you ever played any instruments? Books... I enjoy reading both fiction and nonfiction. Some of my favorite books/authors are The Kite Runner, Jane Austin, and Nora Roberts. I am currently reading Memoirs of a Geisha which is really interesting. I don't know if I told you or not - I also keep a journal. I love to look back over it and just see what and how I was feeling about certain things in my past. I also knit ~ only scarves though for now. I really like to cook - all type of things. Perfume - I usually wear Euphoria by Calvin Klein, also like Romance by Ralph Lauren, and Jean Paul Gautier. I would also like to know the answers to these questions by you.
Also, I would love to hear about your childhood - it is crazy that we are from 2 completely different parts of the world, but yet we seem to have a lot in common. I have really enjoyed getting to know you each day a little more. I hope you have a wonderful Monday and rest of the week. Much happiness, Laurie

Carlo and I began exchanging pictures of our lives. He sent me photos of his home on the island of Sardinia, and I sent him photos of my life in Ohio—quite a contrast, to say the least. I was in awe of Sardinia's white mountains and inviting beaches along an azure sea.

I was also captivated with the way he wrote, charmed by his amusing English yet more stunned by his effortless manner of expressing what he truly felt— and how he connected with me: "It's great hearing how you manage the days, with a little daughter depending on you." I was further reassured of his character as Pamela's family thought so highly of him.

Carlo and I began to write to one another several times a day. I couldn't wait for his next email, and soon we were instant messaging. I shared my daily experiences and all of Sofia's and my activities. I was careful to emphasize how much motherhood meant to me. I wanted there to be no misunderstanding on that front. One day I wrote: "Since Sofia has been in my life, she has added so, so much to every part of who I am. Life can be hard sometimes, but knowing that all the hard work, time, effort will pay off in the end."

I told Carlo about every aspect of my life, even my job at LaScala. I wondered what he would think of the Italian food I served up on weekends. I sent him photos of my family, and pictures of Ohio in every season. Carlo in turn shared his daily routine in Dublin, and in between spoke about his family, friends, and life back in Italy. In one email where he was updating me on his day, he suddenly wrote: "How is it possible? Perhaps through these emails are you becoming the "special someone" to share my daily life with?"

Was that what was happening? I didn't know what to think. It was like a scene right out of that quirky Tom Hanks-Meg Ryan rom-com, *You've Got Mail.* I responded:

Sent: Tuesday, June 03, 2008
Subject: 10 pictures for you

Good Morning Carlo,

I honestly believe that everything happens for some reason - the reason being unknown while experiencing life through the journey. Looking back on life puts so many perspectives on what life is all about. When I was younger I viewed the world, people - everything so differently than I do at the age of 28. I am happy with the direction my life is going, I know who I am, and I have amazing people to share my life with. It seems like I could go on forever and ever sharing thoughts, experiences, and such with you. It seems almost unreal to me at times - going to Ireland, experiencing a whole new world, meeting loads of people, coming back home, evaluating life . . . and now I am getting to know THE guy from Italy who lives in Ireland. The future is unknown. Life is truly amazing.

And he responded:

Sent: Wednesday, June 04, 2008
Subject: 10 pictures for you

Laurie,

Your emails always make me smile and happy and I think this is the best way to begin any day!

Thanks for your thoughts which I share with you at 100% (our common way to think about things...right?!)

I completely agree with you, everything sounds strange and amazing. How two different persons, coming from two opposite parts of the world, with two different lives and experiences seem to have tons of things to be shared. As you wrote and as I already thought during these past days, it seems like we could share our experiences and thoughts for ever and ever.

I'm getting very interested knowing you a little better day after day and it's a thing that always make me happy. THE Girl from Ohio, arrived in Ireland to change my life, has already began to write the happy moments of my new one...

And so, Carlo and I fell into this relationship where we were getting to know one another through our thoughts and our words, rather than through our physical bodies. It was equally as romantic and exciting, and of course much, much more substantial. Carlo mentioned this in one of his emails after we had chatted in real time: "I would have to agree with you about to feel close to you when I write these emails. Several times I find myself writing these lines to you while it seems like you are close to me and I am just speaking with you...we are discovering each day something new about us and all the times it seems as a little brick has been laid to build something huge...."

I was amazed and enamored. The way he spoke from the heart was unlike any man I had ever known. My world began to orbit around two shining stars: Sofia, and Carlo. I wanted to write my thoughts to him with all openness and honesty:

Sent: Friday, June 06, 2008
Subject: 10 pictures for you

Carlo - Hello and Good Morning to You!

I want to start off by saying that it was really nice yesterday getting to chat with you! And then getting a really amazing email. It is crazy how little things like that can be so exciting.

So many times each day I think about you... always happy thoughts! It is just so hard to believe what is happening day after day. I can honestly say that this is an amazing experience to share with you - it feels so real. Without you saying 100% - I understand, feel, think about what that is also. When someone can come into your life and add so much in such a short time, only getting to meet once, and lay the foundation for an amazing friendship aside from everything else. I can feel a very strong connection between us - and this is just email.

When I look back to the evening when I first met you. It was brief - You carried Rita's bag for her up to Kevin's house. And then meeting you the next evening at the Russel's Court Hotel - it seemed so natural for us to hang out that night. When you first arrived we instantly starting chatting. You even stopped at the Chipper - great memories that we can share. Now that I am getting to know you better I am just amazed that I met such an awesome person that night....

Even my journal entries took on a new heightened sense of excitement and awareness:

Journal: Sunday, June 8, 2008

"It has been 8 days since I last wrote and a lot has transpired. Carlo, the Italian that rents from Pamela's uncle Kevin, and I are sharing an amazing experience together. It is hard to even put into words how amazing Carlo is. I always try analyzing things - this was just so unexpected. We shared an amazing evening together at the Russell's Court Hotel and exchanged emails in order to share pictures. One email has turned into a daily email and Carlo is honestly one of the most thoughtful people I have ever met. So sincere and loves life. We share a common way of thinking. 100% Always. Carlo and I discuss life, share photos, and it is so enjoyable getting to share my days with him. Even though our current relationship is online, I feel closer to him than I have ever felt with anyone else. I know he cares, thinks about me, enjoys me in his life. It is all so incredible. Sometimes I have to pinch myself to make sure this is real...."

Our emails were not only documentation of our days, but they became painfully cloying in our desire to meet. It wasn't long before the subject was broached by Carlo himself: "Laurie....I would like to tell you something, something that is crossing my mind almost every day. I think life MUST be lived at 100%, you know this and you agree with me. Knowing you is becoming such an interesting something that I would love to meet you again. I wouldn't have any problem to take a plane to meet my friend in Ohio, but you would have to tell me what you think about this! I never thought about Ohio as the first place to go once in United States and as you can imagine I would go there only to meet you and Sofia. For this reason it is very important that you share with me what you are thinking about this right now. I think today I gave to you something to think about!"

I wrote back and asked him "What are you waiting for?" I was ready to see him again, after two weeks of constant emails. I had to know if the guy I met in Ireland was the same guy who was emailing me. I was certain of his identity, obviously, but I had to put this whole cyber-personality together with the guy in the driveway back in Dublin. It was almost as if Carlo were his own Cyrano.

So it was that Carlo began to make plans for his first trip to the US. In the meantime, our emails were constant, full of discovery and an impassioned desire to be together. My friends had varied reactions. Many were intrigued about my online relationship with a handsome Italian I had only recently met in Ireland. To people in small-town mid-Ohio, this was exotic and the stuff of romance novels. OF course, Pam was in my corner, being a firsthand observer. My parents were their usual guarded selves—not overly skeptical but definitely not surprised by their daughter's rose-colored glasses or her idealistic ideas about romance. Mom and Dad had their "let's wait and see" faces firmly in place. My aunt was a bit more direct. She didn't think Italian men were well-known for treating their women well. I wondered if she had seen *The Godfather* too many times, but I knew she meant well. All would happen in good time—because Carlo was coming to America!

Buongiorno, Tesoro!

C arlo planned his trip for late July, so we had several weeks to keep emailing and getting to know one another. I began listening to the same music he listened to, filling my world with all things Italian. I was even inspired to change my career plans: after hearing so many compliments on my photos of Ireland, I wanted to become a professional photographer. I began to focus on this goal as I continued my other work.

In the meantime, our communications became more intense and our dialogue more unrestrained. One of Carlo's emails in June caught me completely off-guard:

Sent: Monday, June 09, 2008
Subject: 10 pictures for you
Hi Laurie,
Welcome back home after your free evening!
I am sure you had a great time with Pam.
…We can write/speak to each other about hundreds of things, and it always seems as we are thinking in a very similar way, with very similar ideas and thoughts.
When I first met you, I thought you were very good looking and funny, but I saw something in your eyes that I didn't understand. I did not realize what it was, but when our email-relationship started, and it's amazing also the way it suddenly started, I began

to understand that you were not only good looking and funny... I can see into you, tons of lovely things. I really do not know what will happen, but we can be sure that we are enjoying in the best possible way every moment life is presenting to US!

I looked back to my trip to Ireland and thought how oblivious I had been. I was reacting to all that was new, of course, the proverbial "stranger in a strange land" where every moment contained a new experience. I marveled that I was so unaware of this man who had clearly been observing me while I danced the night away with one handsome Irish boy after another.

Carlo and I were in a mutual romantic delirium. It would spill over into our daily interactions with others and we would write about it. In June, I had a client from Italy and I messaged Carlo about it: "Carlo...I am not sure if you will receive this on the phone...I just wanted to tell you that my last client was from Italy. She was so nice - her name was Federica. She was from Venice. I was so excited when she said that she was Italian... She has been in the US for one year, lovely person. I had to deny her all benefits due to her not being a citizen of the US. I wanted so badly to help her - she was so nice! She taught me a few new Italian words - YEAH!"

Carlo in turn was having his own giddy boil-overs in his daily routine: "As I wrote you this afternoon, today I had a chat with my best-colleague in the office. She is 40, married with 2 kids and I love her. She is always very nice with me, and while I am abroad, she always sends me a particular kind of chocolate-candies which I love so much! :). I spoke with her about all this story and it has been very nice. Once I finished, she smiled at me and she only told me "Carlo, what are you doing still here? Run over there and live the Life at its best".

If I didn't have Sofia and my jobs to keep me busy, I don't know what I would have done. I began soliciting photography jobs as well—senior pictures, weddings—all in an effort to make my dream a reality, inspired by my recent Irish dream and its strange turn of events. I was exhilarated, fearless, and exploding with passion about everything. Carlo and I reminded ourselves daily that we were "the lucky ones". My friends and family continued to watch in astonishment, not sure of what to make of this magical, cyberspace balloon that was carrying me off to parts unknown. Was it full of nothing but "hot air"? Or would I land safely in a new place, with a new life, a new love, and new adventures? My journal entries certainly revealed my "cloud nine" status:

Journal: Saturday, June 14, 2008

Life is truly amazing! The experiences that I am having everyday are so WOW WOW WOW WOW WOW WOW! No words can describe how I am feeling every day. Carlo WOW WOW WOW! He has added so much to my daily life. The relationship that we currently have is incredible. I have never experienced anything close to this. The whole meeting, emails, and now we are both enjoying life even more than ever. I love that Carlo likes to live his life at 100%. To share my life with this type of person is amazing. I never knew instant messaging could be some much fun. I love getting to say hello sporadically throughout our days.

In the middle of all the emails, IMs, and brief phone calls, it was decided that, rather than coming straight to Ohio, Carlo would meet me in New York. It would be something right out of *An Affair to Remember*. We needed the private time to connect with one another, obviously, without being under the microscope of my family and friends. We began counting the days, as I revealed in my journal entry in mid-June:

"I am getting to meet Carlo in NYC in a month. How sweet is that! We are going to have an amazing time together. I look forward to just sit next to him. I will most likely be smiling every minute of our time together. He is across the ocean and has changed my life in the most amazing way. Beth, my hairdresser, said that I could not stop smiling when I was telling her about Carlo. I am so thankful for having this opportunity to share these experiences with such an amazing person. So happy."

Carlo became a presence in my life at every breathing moment. I couldn't watch a movie, read a book, or hear a song without thinking of him. I watched the movie *P.S. I Love You* and was awash in yearning at the scenes in Ireland. Later I wrote to Carlo:

"It is crazy how much I am feeling these days. When you said that you have never had an experience nor felt like this before - it is mind blowing the reality of our lives. TRUE HAPPINESS - just getting to share one's life with another. The joy that this can bring to life is GREAT! The past 3 years of my life have been good - being single and getting to experience that life has taught me so much while I have gained so much independence, personal growth, and strength - looking back at the difficult moments that taught me all the important lessons to get where I am today! WOW - it has paid off - I wouldn't trade anything in this world for this experience w/ you."

Any time I met a European in my work, whether at the office or at LaScala, I would gush about Carlo. Somehow it made me feel closer to him. Our blossoming love affair was so surreal, a phenomenon made more poignant when I reviewed my journal entries prior to my trip to Ireland:

Journal: Monday, April 28, 2008

At certain times people come into your life and effect it in ways unimaginable. Everyday is new and unknown! Leaving for Ireland in 16 days-How one experience can change your thoughts and feelings. Another country, culture, experiencing the unknown-all I can say is that it is going to be a totally amazing trip in every possible way. Life changing to be exact!

I noted how I had counted the days before my Irish excursion, and now I was counting the days until my New York adventure. Our emails became so filled with sweet, ardent exaltations that they could make a reader diabetic! We were on a sugar high of romantic discovery. By the time I left for NY, I would address him as *carissimo* and Carlo would address me in his emails as his *tesoro*, his treasure.

We wrote about the *kismet* in our lives that led up to our meeting. Carlo had applied for a passport long before he met me. He was asked if he wanted the kind for travel to the US, and he opted for it, though he had no plans to travel there. I had a friend who had actually traveled to Sardinia, and I kept circling around all things either Italian or Irish—I even ate my lunch at a place called "The Greene". And...the Fourth of July was coming as was my family's annual trip to *Emerald Isle*, North Carolina...the synchronicity was crazy.

As usual I wrote in my journal. On the way to North Carolina with my family, I wrote my thoughts:

Journal: Saturday, June 28, 2008

...Amazing how new experiences in my life help me to have a new appreciation for things. I am so thankful for all my friends and family. I have so many great people in my life. People that truly care about me! I am very happy with life and then add Carlo to the mix. He came to me at a time of life that I am able to fully appreciate all that he is. I look forward to what the future holds. NYC in 27 days. If someone would have told me 6 weeks ago that this was going to be my life I would have not believed it. Today it is my reality.

Carlo has added so much happiness to my life. He and I enjoy each other so much. We are both thinking "HOW?" but loving every minute of the experience. I have never felt or experienced anything like this.

Another cool thing is having our entire relationship documented: 50 emails, tons of chats, and a couple phone calls. It has been so lovely. 100% Sunshine 7c+7d 2 lucky ones. Lovely Laurie. Yours and only for you. Carlo&Laurie. Summer in NY. The girl from Ohio. My Irish Italian Friend. Special person. BLISS. A present made in the USA. Those are some of our common words we share. Truly amazing.

It has been 3 years since going to the Outer Banks, NC. Where I was then vs. now is remarkable. It is a complete 180° change for the better. The last 3 years of my life have taught me so much....

While Sofia and I were on Emerald Isle with the family, we did our usual beach routine and relaxed. I also shared everything about Carlo with my family: his photos, his emails. Everyone was excited for me, but my folks are Midwesterners, and seeing is believing. I knew that it would only be real to them on the day that Carlo arrived in Ohio. They needed to see if Laurie's "pen pal" was more than just a flight of fancy or mad infatuation.

Carlo and I continue to write, discussing everything from his favorite uncle to his love of cars, from Sofia's growth to what my family had for dinner that night. We shared our days as though we weren't thousands of miles apart. I wrote him from Emerald Isle: "I knew that you would understand my feelings in regards to having too much time to just relax. Without me having to explain in so much detail...you just understood - while helping me to feel better, look at the situation with different eyes - I appreciate you for being my special person that just understands me! I love talking with you whenever we get the chance... it adds happy feelings to my days...."

One thing Carlo and I never threw out there was the "L" word. We both knew better than to go there before we became a physical couple. We didn't need it: we were content to bask in what was happening as we shared our words, our thoughts. We were each other's "special person", as I had alluded to that fateful night at the hotel in Dublin.

By the time we got back from North Carolina during the first week of July, the New York trip was coming to fruition. Carlo wrote me in his usual endearing English: "This evening I ended up with the hotel... We will stay in a very nice place, in the center of NY, close to hundreds of things... it's my little surprise for you (one of them), so do not ask me anything about that! I was very excited looking for this place, as it was another brick of the huge bridge we definitely built between US! It sounds strange looking back at some words/sentences used in earlier emails... What in the beginning could be a feeling, day after day has become something really incredible. Something not afraid of the distance, not afraid of 2 different lives lived in 2 different places, something hard to be believed for normal people...."

It was now a matter of a few weeks, days really, before we would meet. I tried to live in the moment every chance I could, but fatal gravity constantly pulled my mind to the near future and what lay ahead. Carlo and I were approaching our hundredth email exchange in between chats and phone calls. It was all I could do not to live the future in my head, instead of looking at what was right in front of me.

Journal: Sunday, July, 13, 2008

"So, 12 days and I will be meeting a person that has added so much positive, happy, lovely, special, real feelings and thoughts to my life! Outside it is pouring. Crazy storm, Rumbling thunder, and a Beautiful light show put on by nature. Carlo has booked the hotel - it's a surprise. This is going to be an out of this world experience. The crazy connection we are feeling is such a great feeling. Enjoying life at all times. Someone that can be a part of this experience with me, in this way.....it's truly incredible. It's Carlo&Laurie! It even just sounds right when said. To be having this experience together and then add US + NY = Amazing! We are going to be enjoying life on another level. I feel so at peace everyday knowing that Carlo is always close to me. He is someone that truly cares - I can feel this. I had a great day today. With Carlo close everything is truly better, happier. How is this possible? Carlo has truly added an amazing feeling to my life. How Amazing! These memories that we are sharing each day will always be remembered as something so special. This experience is unlike any other. Unreal - yet it's reality!"

Only when I held Sofia did I truly come to earth…

"Meet Me at the Top of the Empire State Building—I mean, Starbucks."

Journal: Friday, July 25, 2008 (1:08pm)

Today is the day I've been waiting for!! Currently on the airplane, flying to meet my Carlo. The feelings and emotions are incredible. I am so happy, excited, and anxious. When we first meet I have a very strong feeling...it is going to be a truly amazing moment in my life. Tonight we get to go on our first date: a dinner cruise on the Hudson River. My life has become so amazing since meeting Carlo. Smiling all the time. I could have never imagined such an amazing feeling in which one person can bring to your life. Just 3 years ago - even last year at this time: I was going through my journey - learning, experiencing, and always growing - and now it all makes perfect sense: I was gaining independence, confidence, and a new appreciation for life...having all of this allows me to have so much more to offer MSO (My Special One)! This NY trip with Carlo is something I could have never imaged! Getting to bring Carlo to Ohio is going to be so much fun. Show MSO my life - while getting to experience it with him - sharing the amazing feelings that we do is going to make everything we do so much more amazing. Across an ocean Carlo has made me the happiest I have ever been. Together at last...I have met an incredible person - I am the luckiest girl - and I am so thankful for this entire experience with Carlo Pilia: My Irish Italian special Person who is Always Close to Me (ACTY)! The start of something amazing!!

The day I left for the airport my nerves were raw. I was both excited and a little scared. Before I headed for Columbus, I phoned Pam and told her I needed to meet with her. I drove to where she worked, and she came outside to meet me. We sat on a bench in the shade, out of the hot July sun, and talked about what was about to happen. She was confident and encouraging. She reassured me that all would be well, whatever the outcome. I couldn't help but think of that time she went with me to John's apartment. She had been by my side through all my ups and downs. Pam was my effervescent, blonde fairy godmother: she had helped release me from my tower-prison of a marriage, guided me through the dark forests of relationships, and led me to my Prince Charming in a faraway land.

When I walked off the plane, my thoughts raced and my heart pounded. I searched for Carlo but did not see him anywhere. I sent him a text, telling him that I was standing by the Starbucks—silly, giddy Laurie, not thinking that at JFK there were probably fifty Starbucks! I waited for probably a minute or two, but it seemed like an eternity, so I phoned him. He said he was by a Starbucks as well, but since it clearly wasn't "my" Starbucks, we began to home in on one another as best we could. Finally, as I exited the terminal, there was Carlo walking toward me! *My* Carlo! We embraced so tightly I felt like I might have come out the other side of his muscular frame. He hailed a taxi and we were off on our New York adventure.

I can't believe the taxi driver wasn't singed by the glow emanating from both of us. My face hurt from smiling. After hundreds of emails and phone calls filled with longing, we were together! Though he was in a new country and I was in the Big Apple for the first time, I don't think we took in too much of what was outside the cab's windows. Carlo had his arm around me and we kept looking at one another, as if to reassure ourselves that this was no dream and we were really, finally together.

We arrived at our hotel and checked in. When we got up to our room—yes, *our* room—I was shaking. It was all so amazing, and even though we had spoken every day for weeks, it was still new and somewhat intimidating. We decided to go have coffee—that was safe enough for two people who were crazy for one another but hadn't shared so much as a meal, yet. Before we left the room, Carlo presented me with a beautifully wrapped small box: inside was a necklace, Hermès, with three chains of white, gold, and rose gold. There were two cut-out heart pendants attached, matching the chains, and one of them was engraved with our initials and our favorite saying: *100% Always C&L.* After I put the necklace on, Carlo took me in his arms and kissed me. It was a slow, careful, and gentle kiss, complimented by his strong embrace. I felt all the emotion of the past two months converge in one moment.

I also gave him a gift: a photo book that I had made on *Shutterfly.* It was sort of a small scrapbook of our story thus far, with photos and quotes from our conversations.

We went to a small diner across the street from the hotel. Over coffee, we talked about everybody and everything: Sofia, Sardinia, Ireland, our families, our present—and our future. We passed the afternoon getting acclimated to one another's auras. Soon, it was time to get ready for our first night on the town: Carlo had booked a dinner cruise on the Hudson.

Carlo was dressed in his suit and tie and I in my "little black dress". We took a cab to the boat ramp and, after snapping a photo of the two of us, boarded. As if the romance fairies were still toying with us, we were seated next to a nice Irish couple on holiday. We had a lovely conversation with them as we ate, drank, and danced the night away. Of course, the smiles never faded.

We capped off the evening by cruising past the Statue of Liberty. I think I should have been more in awe of the Lady in the Harbor, but truthfully, I kept my eyes on my handsome Italian. This was a dream that had consumed my life because of one spontaneous decision to attend a birthday party a few thousand miles away. I was mesmerized.

I did pause to take a photo of us in that moment and send it to Pamela. She messaged me that it brought tears to her eyes. She was elated for us and couldn't wait to see us when we got to Ohio.

We ended up walking back to our hotel, taking in the city at night with all its sights, sounds, and smells. From the brackish smell of the harbor, to the café-lined streets, through the smoky haze outside the nightclubs, Carlo and I strolled along in the warm night, starstruck. I can't lie that I wasn't a little apprehensive over what the rest of the evening would bring. No longer was there the comfortable distance of email. Carlo's deep, amber eyes were real, inches from my own. He was there, squeezing my fingers in his strong grip, making me feel a little, well, worshiped—in a way I'd never experienced. I think there were moments I stopped breathing.

When we were back in our hotel room, despite an earlier cocktail or two, my spine was rigid and I was locked into Carlo's gaze. When he took me in his arms and kissed me, our lips fit together in a soft, perfect close. He pressed my body to his, enveloping me in an embrace that I could only describe as sweet shelter. The subtle pheromones of CK cologne seduced areas of my brain I didn't know existed. It was like the floor dropped out from beneath me and I was in free-fall.

Carlo was the most sensitive, intuitive, tender lover a man could be: up to that time, I had only been with fumbling, selfish boys. Carlo was a man, albeit a young man, but a man nonetheless in every sense. He had a maturity and a connectivity like I had never experienced with the opposite sex. Of course, we were just getting to know one another, and intimate relationships take time to find their rhythm. I awoke the next morning in Carlo's arms with feelings of both serenity and apprehension. As he held me, whispering words of appreciation and worship, I had so many thoughts running through my head. My endorphins were surging beyond the solar system and I feared the return to earth. After all, we had two weeks of togetherness left...and he still hadn't met my family, nor I his. Was this really the stuff that lasts? It felt like it could be, but all I could do was let Carlo take my hand and lead me. Somehow, I knew I could trust him.

After a languorous morning, we became typical tourists. After breakfast at the hotel, we wandered down Fifth Avenue. Carlo wanted to buy me another gift, but I refused. I wanted to be wooed with more than just "things". It was so important for me to know that whatever this was, it was based on more than material desires. I was quiet as we rode in a carriage through Central Park. I was on sensory overload as I tried to focus on what it meant to *be* with this intriguing and confident man.

Later, we toured the MOMA and went to the NBA store. It turned out Carlo was a huge fan. We both laughed as we placed our instantly dwarfed hands inside Shaquille O'Neal's handprint.

We couldn't miss the opportunity of a Broadway show, so we got tickets for *Chicago*. When I called to get the tickets, I put them under Carlo's name. It was the first time I had said his last name, and I struggled with the pronunciation a bit.

Carlo enjoyed the performance, although I could tell he didn't understand all the words. A musical is more music and action than just words—the American answer to opera—so he smiled through it all. At the end of our evening, we "grabbed a slice", as they say. I found New York pizza to be everything that legend held.

The next morning, I awoke with a calm, happy feeling. Something had clicked, and my nervousness had vanished. Carlo had pre-booked a helicopter ride over Manhattan—I doubt we even needed the helicopter. We were flying high on our own. Afterward, we visited the New York Stock Exchange and had a simple lunch at a nearby café—for a not so simple price, I might add. As we ate, we talked further about our future together, everything that we desired or hoped for.

After lunch it was off to the National Museum of the American Indian. After an enlightening cultural lesson for both of us, we went back to the hotel. Later that evening, we grabbed sushi with my mother's brother, Matt, and his fiancée Carina. They talked about their wedding plans the following May, and teasingly invited both of us if we were "still together" by then. Carlo and I exchanged smiles on that one.

Matt asked Carlo if he drove a Maserati back in Italy. Carlo chuckled. It was the first of many moments where I learned that Americans had many misguided presumptions about Italians, largely due to movies and stories of mafia dons.

The four of us went to a pub after dinner and had a few cocktails, took some photos, and called it a night. It was our last evening in New York. Tomorrow, it was off to the Midwest: I was taking my Sardinian lover to the place of fast food, pre-fab housing, Ohio State football (American football, that is) and Lite beer. All I could do was take a deep breath and get on the plane...

How Do You Say
"Buckeye" in Italian?

At breakfast the next morning, I ordered oatmeal. Carlo thought I had said "omeo" and continued to think that was what it was called for some time afterward (it became a running joke later on).

We headed for the airport—but not before we did some quick souvenir shopping and bought matching NYC t-shirts. When we arrived at the airport our flight was delayed two hours, but we didn't care in the least. One of the flight attendants commented she had never seen two people so happy that their flight was late. It was true: we were so enchanted with one another that nothing could break the spell.

We landed in Columbus that afternoon, located my car and headed for home. I was so anxious to show Carlo my world. He had mentioned that he wanted to try "American fast food". The irony wasn't lost on me that I was once again taking my man to a drive-thru—on the way to meet my daughter. But this time, it was different: really, *really* different. I took him to an Arby's—and he loved it. He was having a "real American experience". I found it amusing since Carlo was a bodybuilder and took great care in what he ate.

My parents had kept Sofia, so we had to meet my mother at our usual meet-up spot in Cincinnati. Sofia smiled through the car window as we drove up. I was so happy to see my little blonde angel. My mother was cordial and rather relaxed to meet my new handsome Italian boyfriend.

It so happened that her brother, my uncle Matt, had emailed her from NYC to tell her that he "approved".

We put Sofia in the car and headed for my place near Dayton. Sofia, who was always outgoing and loved people, was captivated with Carlo. After all, it wasn't like I had exposed her to a lot of guys. He presented her with an adorable pink "girly" purse he had purchased in Ireland. Of course, he was an instant hit. Carlo readily engaged her in conversation, and it was rather amusing as I drove along, thinking that they were learning English together. Carlo later commented that he perfected his English skills by conversing with my three-year-old.

I explained to Sofia that Carlo would be staying at our house for a few days. She was excited to have a houseguest, as was demonstrated when we arrived home: she proceeded to show Carlo her room, along with every doll, toy, and stuffed animal she owned. Carlo was patient and accommodating, which more than impressed Mommy. We relaxed after our long weekend. After I tucked Sofia in that evening, it felt surreal to have Carlo there, in my modest little duplex in small town Ohio—but it felt right.

The next morning, we had breakfast and were content to just hang around my place, playing with Sofia. We were gearing up for our big trip the following day to King's Island amusement park near Cincinnati— where Carlo would officially meet my parents.

As we relaxed that day, Carlo lay on my sofa and when I walked by, he asked me to join him. He pulled me close. *"Ti Amo Moltissimo,"* he said softly. My heart skipped a beat: I spoke no Italian, but I recognized the word "love". For months, this word had been hovering in the background, getting lodged in our throats—and now it was spoken.

I beamed as I lay back in his arms and cherished the moment.

#

Carlo didn't know how to take the idea of meeting my father for the first time at an amusement park. He would have preferred a more formal meeting, something more in line with his European ways. This was a big "Welcome to America, Y'all" for my refined Sardinian. (It would have served no purpose to explain that King's Island was minutes from the Ohio River and the Kentucky border. The catchphrase of "fun for the whole family" would be lost on Carlo. I'm sure he observed a panoply of cultural behaviors that day). Though we were to spend the day on rollercoasters and on water rides, he refused to meet my parents wearing swim trunks. Instead, he wore a dress shirt and trousers. Years later, my conservative Midwestern father would chuckle and say that he feared that, being Italian, Carlo would show up to the park in a Speedo.

Sofia enjoyed the water rides with her grandparents. We all ate lunch together and had a nice visit. Carlo and I waited in a few long lines and rode the park's famous rollercoasters, though I soon discovered my stomach wasn't like it used to be. I was nauseated the rest of the day.

As I said, my Uncle Matt had allayed my parents' fears about "Laurie's new boyfriend" from afar. I could sense that my dad wasn't thrilled that I'd spent the weekend with a man I barely knew—in the same hotel room. He was polite and pleasant, but he was still my father. He observed Carlo closely that day and would later remark that Carlo's comfortable demeanor with Sofia was reassuring.

My mother remained quiet and observant in her own way. She knew her adventurous daughter was picky when it came to men. I think my mom trusted me to put a good man in Sofia's life.

The three of us got back to my place and after a day in the hot sun we were ready to relax in the cool air of my duplex. Sofia was exhausted from all the activity and went to bed with little prompting. When Carlo made love to me that night, there was a moment when I began to cry. He paused, concerned, and asked if I was ok. What could I say? That I had never had a man be so considerate of me as a woman before?

That I had never experienced a lover's generosity with his body as well as his heart? In a rush of indescribable and overwhelming emotion, I told him that I loved him.

#

The real world came crashing into my dream soon enough as I had to return to work, though I was only working half-days. I was a little concerned about what Carlo would do with his time alone, but he discovered Panera. He would drop me off at Job and Family Services and head to Panera with his laptop. Carlo became a "regular" during that fourteen days. One of the staff supplied him with free coffee, and he would converse with the other local Daytonians. Other times, he enjoyed sitting near the (fireless—it was high summer) fireplace and reading his book.

My ten-year class reunion occurred during Carlo's visit. I had a graduating class of only sixty or so people, so the affair was relatively small. The people who showed up were largely those who had never left the area. Many already had families. It was a non-descript, outdoor country potluck. Carlo was expecting something a bit more formal or celebratory: people hugging, all excited to see one another. Suffice to say that few had left their high school cliques. My classmates looked at Carlo as if he were some sort of alien. It was a fun experience for both of us.

One day, Carlo, Sofia, and I went to a local park. Carlo and I played a little one-on-one basketball—we had both played when we were younger. We had so much fun that afternoon. Another day, we did a canoe trip near Springfield. At the risk of conjuring up images of something out of the movie *Deliverance*, I must mention here that this was Carlo's first interaction with those who are typically referred to as "rednecks". These rednecks, however, had an Italian flag on their canoe, which prompted animated conversation when they found out Carlo was the real deal. Carlo loved the group and their twangy accents. I had to translate for both sides at times, as they struggled with Carlo's accent as much as he struggled with theirs.

One of my favorite moments during Carlo's visit was when we were dining at a casual pub near The Greene. The waitress brought Carlo a refill on his Coke, and he immediately became irritated that he was being charged for a drink he did not order. I had to explain the American tradition of "free refills". We both had a good laugh.

Another day was spent with Baca, her husband Charles, and all the grandkids in Miamisburg. I had explained to Carlo how, though she was part of Sofia's biological father's family, she had been a critical source of support in our lives. The kids swam in the pond while Baca drove us around her property in her golf cart. Later we ate "American pizza". It was a memorable summer day.

I took Carlo to the artisan enclave known as Yellow Springs. We started off at Dino's, a great place for coffee, and then strolled around exploring all the different shops. We had a "brush with celebrity" as we passed Dave Chapelle that day. We then ventured over to John Bryan State Park, where we hiked the pine forest and did some rock climbing. Carlo was getting a good dose of Ohio flora and fauna.

I should mention that we did see Pam during Carlo's visit. We all went out for pizza one evening. Pam was happy for us and excited to see Carlo, but she preferred to make herself scarce so that we could have time together.

It soon came time for an evening at LaScala. All my old co-workers were excited to meet my new man. They had heard so much about him, it was time that they knew he was real. That evening was a wild one: we drank and danced the night away. The bartender was intrigued with Carlo's accent, and Carlo had a little fun telling him he was part of the mob (Carlo remembers wearing his Versace suit and red tie and feeling way over-dressed). We ended up at a Bob Evans for breakfast the next morning, wearing our matching NY t-shirts. Carlo and I stayed at my friend Jaime's place.

I was delirious with happiness…but a goodbye was just around the corner.

Arrivederci, Baby—For Now

We had tried not to think about Carlo's trip to America as finite—but of course it was. On that last day, we clung to one another. The drive to the airport was a quiet one. The photo we snapped before he boarded his plane said it all: our expressions, while we struggled to smile, looked more like we were facing a firing squad. I drove home to Dayton that day feeling like I was missing all my limbs. Panic overwhelmed me as I wondered how we would manage being so far apart. I tried to remind myself that Carlo was my love and I was his, and somehow, we would make this work—yet the separation anxiety was excruciating. What was I going to do without my Carlo's arms around me for who knew how long?

We were back to our routine of emailing and video-chatting. It was comforting to hear his voice and look into his eyes, but the yearning to be together was still painful for both of us. Knowing that he cared so much made the separation bearable for me. The big question, obviously, was "What next?"

Pamela was planning another trip to Ireland. She was exploring the possibility of returning to her homeland permanently. I wanted so badly to accompany her, but it just wasn't possible at the time.

But, "love conquers all", as they say, and by the end of August I had booked my next European vacation: I was going to Sardinia in October to meet the Pilia family. Carlo reminded me that his family did not speak

English. It was up to me to learn the *lingua franca*—and at that point I knew three phrases: *Mi piace molto* (I like it a lot); *Mi fai impazzire* (You make me crazy), *Ti Amo Moltissimo* and of course, "spaghetti" and "pizza". I began to study Italian and practice with Carlo.

Meanwhile, I couldn't live in the romantic dreams inside my head all the time. Sofia's life was moving along as well, and I had to keep up. I enrolled her in gymnastic lessons, and she took to it with all the exuberance of a fearless three-year-old with a limber body. I also searched for fun activities to do together. We would go to Young's Dairy and feed the goats. Afterward we would get ice cream. We would also visit Pamela at the stables where she worked (True to her Irish blood, Pamela loved horses).

Sofia was becoming quite the little lady. I was proud that I had one of those children you could take anywhere. It was no surprise. We had been forced to "adapt" together several times since her birth.

In between Sofia and work, I longed for Carlo and counted the days until October 24th. I had a co-worker who had a spouse who worked for an airline company and I managed to get a round-trip ticket to Rome for six-hundred dollars. I couldn't believe my ongoing luck. I must have been kidnapped by alien leprechauns while in Ireland and unwittingly had a four-leaf clover implanted in some part of my anatomy. I was to meet Carlo in Rome, and we would go on to Sardinia.

I studied my Italian in between countless, gushing, exuberant emails and messages from Carlo. He had begun referring to himself tongue-in-cheek as "Old, Bald Carlo"—a reference to my mistaking him for being older than he was the first day I saw him. We stayed in constant contact, still giddy with elation at our finding each other. Our messages were riddled with bold caps and exclamation points of unbridled joy and anticipation.

When the big day of my next European adventure arrived, I couldn't get to the Cincinnati airport fast enough. I took Sofia to Baca's, gave her lots of goodbye kisses and told her I would bring her presents.

She was happy to be spoiled by her doting great-grandmother, along with my parents, for the time being. When I arrived in Rome at 10:45 in the morning, I was bewildered in my unfamiliar surroundings. I thought perhaps I had exited the wrong terminal. People rushed by me, speaking Italian and probably French, Greek, or Farsi for all I knew. Grabbing my phone, I was about to contact someone who could get a message to Carlo when I heard a voice behind me say, "Are you looking for someone?" My heart was in my throat as I spun around and saw my handsome "bald" Italian. I leaped into his arms.

It was Carlo's turn to guide me in a foreign land. We caught a flight to Sardinia and when we arrived Carlo drove us in his company BMW to his family's home. I marveled at the narrow roads and ancient stucco structures that lined the rocky coastlines. As an American, whose country's structures are "new" by world standards, I was enchanted with the yet to be discovered centuries of vast cultural influence before me: pre-historic, Spanish, Moorish, and of course Roman. I breathed the salt air and looked out at a sun-drenched, exotic diamond surrounded by azure seas.

Carlo's family lived close to the capital city of Cagliari in a suburb known as Assemini. Their home was situated on a narrow side street, part of a string of similar structures. Midwestern Americans take their acreage for granted. I was stunned that the home sat right along the street, with no frontage or sidewalk. The modest home where Carlo had grown up had once belonged to his entrepreneur grandfather who, like many Italians throughout history, specialized in stonework and masonry. He had also owned a bakery.

Carlo's mother, Vittoria, met us at the door, her face awash in warmth. She welcomed us into the foyer, where I admired the three generations-old Sardinian chest and the wall tapestry in a cork frame, made—I found out later—by Carlo's grandfather. I was also introduced to his father, Daniele, and his sister, Selena or "Selli", who was soon to graduate from law school. Daniele, in his fifties, was like Carlo in that he enjoyed keeping fit, running and playing tennis. Vittoria was the consummate homemaker, and very proud of their "back garden", a small concrete terrace where she had planted and potted all sorts of exotic flowers, trees, and bushes. We hung out in the kitchen over espresso and some light fare. I just smiled a lot as Carlo translated.

After our brief visit, Carlo and I went to get settled in the apartment where we were staying. A friend of his, Franco, had loaned it to us for my visit. Three days prior to my arrival, there had been a major flood—autumn is the rainy season. It was necessary to check on the apartment and make sure we wouldn't need water-wings. All was well. After we got situated, had a little private time where I had to nearly pinch myself at intervals that I wasn't dreaming, we were off once again to have dinner with the family.

Carlo's mother had prepared a delectable meal of pasta with crème and mushrooms, bread, pastries, assorted meats and coffee. She, Daniele, and Selli all took great pains to make me feel welcome. Though conversations took longer than normal, I could tell during some long pauses that Carlo's family was happy for him. They were close-knit and demonstrably affectionate, and I could see that, whatever was in their son's or brother's heart, that they knew him well enough to share in his joy.

On the way back to the apartment that evening, we detoured through the city. After a brief tour of the port and the beach, we ended the evening at a seaside club called Casi Café, a nightclub with low white couches and a DJ. We had a couple of drinks and danced to the beat of Latin rhythms.

I awoke at eight-thirty the next morning, dragging a bit due to jet lag. We had breakfast at a café overlooking the ocean before going shopping for a graduation present for Selli. I admired all the petite, tan Sardinians walking about in their designer clothes and accessories. In the meantime, I stood out like the proverbial sore thumb, being 5'8", which is tall by Sardinian standards—and blonde. I took in the quaint, narrow streets of Cagliari and all the small cars motoring by. The ancient, sun-baked buildings were enchanting and evocative of long ago.

We had lunch at the Pilia residence. I realized I was going to have to learn to pace myself through the endless courses and rich food. It was wonderful to experience a meal as a social, sensual experience rather than as some brief, uneventful, and ofttimes unhealthy physical necessity. Meanwhile, Carlo's family continued to reach out and get to know me. His mother had learned to say, "Carlo funny". It was so sweet. The language barrier was challenging at times, but Carlo led the way: he simply took over, as tour guide, translator, facilitator, all of it. After an impressive lunch of lasagna, stuffed chicken, bread, potatoes, pastry, and coffee, Carlo and I took a much-needed two-hour nap.

After we freshened up, it was time to pick up Carlo's cousins Andrea and Stefania and have dinner. This was a whole new challenge to my palate: mussels, oysters, grouper, frittata, seabass, linguine with clams, and *bottarga*, the signature Sardinian delicacy of dried roe from either tuna or mullet. It is most generally grated onto pasta but is also sliced and eaten with a little olive oil. To my chagrin, I was the sort of person who had a limited food repertoire: fast food kids' meals with chicken nuggets and barbecue sauce. Pamela often teased me over it. That evening was the beginning of my culinary education.

Carlo asked me about eating pasta with a "sponge"—he meant "spoon". I was charmed as usual. After coffee and sorbet with strawberries, I was stuffed. So much food!

We took the cousins home and then went out to a disco club where Carlo used to work. We danced, met some of Carlo's friends and had a fun time. I was amused that there was American music playing, but no one spoke English. Music, as a language, is universal. Later, I was also intrigued when I turned on a television at the apartment and observed all the American shows with Italian voice-overs.

The third day of my Sardinian adventure consisted of lunch at Carlo's parents' house and then football—not soccer, but American football, which Carlo loved—in the yard situated beyond the terrace. At one point, Daniele told me to "sit down", in English, and Carlo reminded him to say, "Sit down, please." Daniele wanted to be polite and offer me a seat and when he later found out that his English gesture could be interpreted differently, he felt embarrassed. I was touched by how they were trying to reach out and speak my language.

After an invigorating afternoon, Carlo and I did some shopping and took some photos in Cagliari before heading for the beach. I took in the rocky coastlines, the white sands, and water in shades of blue that were not yet in my vocabulary to describe. Afterward, we went to Carlo's friend Franco's house. There were three other couples in attendance, along with two children. Of course, there was also more incredible food, accompanied by wine and *limoncello*. The "liquid inspiration" resulted in my relaxing and trying out my Italian: *"molto vino"*, *"parlo molto Italiano"*, *"Vieni, Carlo"*, *"sogni doro"*, *"Buona Notte"*, *"molto bacio"*, *"Si certo"*, *"Eja"*. It was a wonderful evening full of fun and laughter. I was taken with Carlo's friends and how much they cared about him.

The next day, a Monday, we woke up early. After a breakfast of pastries and tea, it was off to Selli's graduation. We joined Carlo's family and a couple of friends and sat down in a room with a panel of ten professors. Selli was the seventh person to be called. She spoke to the panel for eight minutes and then we all left the room. When we re-entered a short time later, she received her passing grade. A flurry of pictures, well-wishes, flowers, and gifts ensued. Carlo presented her with a diamond necklace.

After the celebration, Carlo and I went to his office to meet some of his co-workers. People were very gracious and those who could speak English to me did. Then, Carlo whisked me off to Assemini, to a small shop that sold sunglasses. The proprietor recognized Carlo immediately and minutes later Carlo had bought me my first pair of *nice* sunglasses—Gucci. After some more time at the beach, followed by a stop at a small café where Carlo and I took some time to talk, it was time to attend Selli's open house.

It was also my "grand introduction" to Grandma and various aunts and cousins. The family all lived nearby. Everyone was so kind. We were then off to dinner with Carlo's best friend Giosue at Pizza Palace. When Carlo asked me what I wanted on my pizza, I politely responded, "Oh, whatever everyone else is having"—not knowing that in Italy, everyone gets their own pizza—no sharing! Italian pizza dances on the palate—the thin crust delivers the dynamic toppings without overwhelming your appetite. It is the real deal!

Giosue had a devilish sense of humor. He told me to say, *"De pressi!"* to the waitress, which means, "Make it fast!" in Sardinian. The waitress was not impressed with my unintended imperiousness. I also tried escargot that evening—not my favorite. At the end of dinner there were rounds of *Mirto*, a Sardinian liqueur distilled from myrtle berries.

The following day, my fifth day in Sardinia, Carlo and I packed our bags for a trip around the island. After stopping at his family's place for some food and other items for the trip, we were off to Olbia. At a gas station along the way, I practiced my Italian/Sardinian. I managed not much more than "Nice to meet you" and "Bye" to a couple of elderly ladies in the restroom, but I was proud of myself for trying.

On the road, I gazed out at the white mountains, at sheep grazing on hillsides, and the occasional tiny car that passed us. We stopped several times to take pictures. Soon we arrived at Costa Smeralda, an area known to be patronized by elites and their yachts. It was off-season so the place was deserted. Carlo and I had the beach to ourselves. The water was crystal blue: I could see through to the sandy bottom. It was breathtaking. After lunch at a seaside café, we traveled to the coastal resort of Stintino, where Carlo's family owned a beach house. Carlo took me out for yet another fabulous dinner and then we retired.

We had set our alarm for 4:30am as we wanted to watch the sunrise. We got up and got dressed, but as soon as we were about to go outside, a storm rolled in. Back to bed! Finally, we got up around 10:30 and had some breakfast. I was captivated with yet more white sand, mountains, and the cerulean sea. Once again, we had the place to ourselves. Carlo carried me down the beach on his back. My emotions at that moment were indescribable: I was the living embodiment of the cover of a romance novel.

When we arrived back in Assemini, Vittoria presented me with a coffee set and asked me to "please remember her". Selli gave me a beautiful necklace. I truly was falling in love with this amazing family. Carlo indulged me further by buying me a new winter coat at Benetton. Later, we had dinner with cousins Andrea and Stefania at their home: pizza, followed by lemon cake and limoncello. It was another enchanted evening, but my heart was growing heavy as my trip would soon be ending.

The next day, I did some shopping for Sofia and my family. I bought Sofia a "Dora" book in Italian—she loved to read—and got my parents a Sardinian cookbook. I picked up things for Baca, Pam, and a few others. We had lunch with the Pilia family. Selli arrived home from her first day of work as a lawyer. Then, it was off to the airport to catch a flight to Rome. After arriving in Rome, we visited Carlo's high school friend Simone and had another great pizza dinner at his apartment.

The next morning, we awoke at 4am so I could catch my flight back to the States. I held onto Carlo the whole time in the car. Another goodbye was imminent, and I was near tears. "Don't worry," he reassured me, "this is just the beginning of an amazing life together." All I could think of was the fifty-seven days it would be until I would see my Carlo again. Could I endure another separation? Could *we* endure it?

What I didn't know, and wouldn't until much, much later, was that three months prior, on our first night in New York, Carlo had texted his mother: *Get ready. She's the one...*

Christmas Snow, Christmas Stress, or "Yule" Never Guess Who Showed Up at Grandma's

I arrived home safely after my stand-by flight and was so happy to hug my Sofia and give her her gifts. She had celebrated Halloween with my parents and had a great time. My parents were excited to hear about my trip but, looking back, I'm sure they wondered what all this would mean. Their daughter had fallen in love with a man who lived in one country and worked in another. How was this going to end up?

Carlo and I continued to talk every day, either by email, SKYPE, or instant message. I do admit that the distance made me nervous at times. When I would phone Carlo and he wouldn't answer, I'd get a sense of panic. My fears were residual baggage from my earlier relationship. It was silly, as he always contacted me routinely and never gave me a reason to doubt him. I had fallen so precipitously, however, that I worried that our time apart would somehow kill the passion. Then, I'd get a message like this:

You already know that I always do what I desire to do—so baby, get ready! Yours, Carlo.

I had also written a long, heart-felt letter to Carlo's family. I wrote it in Italian and had Carlo assist me in the translation, which was a good thing: at one point in the letter, I had expressed my being excited to meet them, but I had used the word for being sexually excited. Carlo and I had a good laugh over that near- disaster. I did express my deepest gratitude for their warmth and generosity. I told them that seeing where Carlo came from made me love him all the more.

After my Sardinian island adventure, it was hard to adjust to life once more in the stark November landscape of Ohio. I kept prosciutto, pancetta, and a good selection of cheese in my fridge—and I drank espresso in my demitasse. *And*, I had to get back to work, both at the social services office and at the restaurant. Of course, I had Pamela to share everything with. She continued to be happy for me as my relationship with Carlo blossomed.

There was another piece of reality, though, that had only been a fleeting specter in the back of my mind. I had drowned it out with Sardinian sunshine, but it reared its ugly head in full force when I returned home.

My daughter's father.

Well, not exactly him, but it might as well have been. Since Sofia was born, I had maintained good relationships with both Baca, my ex's grandmother, as well as his mother. I wanted Sofia to know all her grandparents. My former mother-in-law and I had been in close contact since my divorce. She spent lots of time with Sofia and often was my choice for childcare.

One day, not long after I had returned home from Sardinia, Sofia came home from her grandmother's and mentioned, in her three-year-old way of communicating, that she had seen her father (she referred to him by name) at her "mamaw's house" and he "did not even say hello". He had been there to drop off his older daughter.

I was immediately alarmed. Up to that point Sofia had spent zero time with her biological father. She didn't know him. Forget the fact that

I got no child support. Add his disturbing history to all of this, and I was more than worried. I won't deny, either, that I was thinking of the various ways my future with Carlo could go—and it would be very easy for my ex to make our lives miserable. And now, his mother appeared to be facilitating it.

From the beginning, Sofia's grandmother had been supportive of my leaving her son. But, "blood is thicker than water", right? I had no doubt that, now that I was seeing this exotic stranger from another land, being whisked off and showered with gifts, that fear, jealousy, and resentment would arise. I could justify some of her fear—she loved Sofia and the thought of her perhaps moving away to another country was no doubt scary. Still, she knew how I felt about Sofia being around her father without my supervision or consent.

The depth of her about-face was revealed to me when I confronted her. "I desire Sofia to have a relationship with [John]," she said, "and I am happy to facilitate it at my house. If I were [John] I would be taking you to court to get rights... [John] has been asking about Sofia over the years."

My response was swift and direct: "If John wants to be a part of her life after all these years then he needs to call *me*. He needs to make the effort—not you."

So much for my Sardinian island afterglow. The safe little cocoon in which I had ensconced Sofia and myself was being penetrated by a swarm of hornets. My heart pounded as I envisioned lawyers, custody battles, and, worst of all, being tethered to Sofia's father in some bogus parental relationship that for him didn't exist at all—unless it suited his current ego trip. I was forced to be more cautious when it came to my relationship with Sofia's paternal grandmother. I tried to put the rest of it out of my mind and look forward to Christmas, when Carlo would arrive for the holiday.

Carlo arrived on the twenty-seventh of December, after spending Christmas with his family. We celebrated Christmas at my parents' house. Sofia made quite a haul from Santa and co: princess clothes, Snow White tickets, and passes to an indoor waterpark, just to name a few presents. Carlo brought me a special present all the way from Ireland—a Burberry bag and wallet. I had no idea about this designer. I later saw the price and nearly fainted. I was so happy to be with all the people I adored. I could not have imagined a more perfect Christmas.

Sofia and Carlo were forming their own bond as well. She was becoming accustomed to him being in our lives, either via SKYPE calls or during his visits. When they weren't playing some sort of game, the three of us would cuddle on my sofa. I think Sofia sensed my newfound happiness and in her own child-like way welcomed it. I never sensed any resentment or jealousy when it came to Mommy dividing her affections.

Carlo and I celebrated New Year's Eve at LaScala. I worked until around 10:30 that evening. Carlo sat at a table and patiently waited for me. My parents, Lynn, and Pamela all came in closer to midnight. We rang in the New Year with toasts and dancing. I think my parents were becoming more enamored with Carlo by the minute. Maybe it was just the glow on their daughter's face at that point, but I think they were getting an idea of Carlo's integrity and character as well.

On this trip, Carlo got to experience another strange American tradition: the after-Christmas sales. He said he had never experienced anything like it, as it wasn't a European "thing".

For a romantic getaway, I rented a cabin in Kentucky. Not exactly exotic Stintino, but exotic for Carlo in any case. We were nestled in the snow-covered hills next to a roaring fire…and we had a hot tub to boot.

We had one near-tragedy when I took Carlo skiing. Pamela and her friend Neil met us at a ski lodge in Bellefontaine, Ohio. It was only my third time skiing, but it wasn't the Alps or Breckenridge, right? It was mid-Ohio. Carlo had never skied, so we started on the "bunny hill"—and it really is a hill. There are no mountains in Ohio, just in case the reader is geographically unfamiliar.

I showed Carlo how to "snow-plow" and after a brief lesson, we started down the hill. I began to pick up speed, assuming Carlo was behind me and would meet me at the foot of the slope. When I got to the bottom: no Carlo.

I stood waiting and looking up the hill for some time and finally, a person appeared, carrying their skis and limping along. It was my handsome Italian, and he had a look of panic on his face.

"I almost died!" he exclaimed.

Carlo told me that he had skied up to a place where the snowbank ended. He could not stop and had jumped to avoid some rocks. He ended up tumbling through the woods and injuring his shoulder. His jacket was ripped and he was in a lot of pain.

I felt terrible. Here was Carlo, in a foreign country with no health insurance. I should never have taken him skiing, or at least not without a lesson or two from someone instead of novice like me. He refused to go and get checked out. In the end, he was ok, with no serious injury. I will never forget that day and how badly I felt.

We ended our holiday respite with a trip to Yellow Springs where we walked through the quiet, snow-covered village and spent some time talking and just being together. We kissed goodbye once more, but this time not for long: a Valentine's Day reunion in Chicago was in our sights.

Winds of Change in the Windy City

It is of course no surprise that during our holiday time Carlo and I had begun talking seriously about our future together. Obviously, an ocean between us was a huge encumbrance and a financial strain. We had to set some workable plans in motion.

Acquiring work visas for either of us was difficult if not time-consuming. We talked a little about our options over Christmas, but Chicago, the "City of the Big Shoulders", to quote Sandburg, got my big-shouldered Italian in a decisive mood.

What a romantic, albeit freezing, good time we had! After another long, airport embrace, it was off in a taxi to all that Rush and Division, Navy Pier, the Aquarium and the Art Institute had to offer.

At the Aquarium, I saw for the first time Carlo's passion for sea life. I watched his eyes light up as he gazed at every jellyfish and ray, studying them with intensity. He could have stayed there for days. He pored over the information and enjoyed discussing aquatic life in detail.

I myself loved the Natural History and Art Museums, the latter's tiny house exhibit being something I'll never forget. We took a double-decker bus tour as well, taking in the city. We were bundled up like Eskimos. I think only my eyes were exposed the entire trip.

Carlo introduced me to another of his passions: like many Italians, he loves opera. I must say I loved the "getting dressed up" part and all the ceremony of it all, but I was in no way bawling my eyes out like Julia

Roberts in *Pretty Woman*. I dozed off during the Portuguese folk opera. Fortunately, Carlo was forgiving. At the risk of being called a rube, my most vivid memory of that evening was the Chicago-style pizza we had later.

We no sooner wiped the pizza sauce from the corners of our lake-effect chapped lips than we had to say goodbye once more. When I got home, I found a note from Carlo in the pocket of my coat: *I am so thankful to share my life with someone so special.*

#

Journal: Sunday, February 22, 2009

Everything in life happens for a reason and a purpose. Enjoy the ride while making the most of each new day.

After the strain of another farewell, Carlo and I were ready to be on the same continent together permanently. It made the most sense for Sofia and me to move to Ireland. Carlo was part-owner of his engineering company in Dublin, and I had dreamt of living in Ireland, after all. But there were hurdles at every turn. In the end, graduate school was our best hope: for me, a student visa was the easiest.

Carlo and I began researching colleges and universities in Dublin. I really had to lean on him for help, as my Dublin experience had been one hazy, long weekend of a party—not exactly a guided tour. I ended up applying to two schools: University College Dublin and Dublin University, majoring in Human Resource Management. After my work in Social Services, I knew I wanted to remain on the "people side" of business. As I filled out applications and wrote essays, I couldn't believe where the last seven months of my life had taken me—and where I was going, it seemed.

During this time, I read Elizabeth Gilbert's *Eat, Pray, Love*. Readers will recall that Elizabeth's journey began in Italy. I loved reading the Italian phrases and memorizing them so that I could repeat them to

Carlo. Gilbert's book made me so excited for my future. Like her, I was embarking on a journey of discovery and passion.

I was of course living in the now as well. I saw six to eight welfare clients each day. As I listened, I appreciated that everyone takes, and makes, their own journey. I also loved my cubicle mate, my co-worker Arlene. She was always eager for "Carlo and Laurie" updates and was a huge supporter of my plans and dreams. Pamela was always there as well. We grabbed lunch, went shopping, got mani-pedis as I waited for news from Ireland.

When spring began to thaw the frozen cornfields, I decided to start running again. I hadn't for some time, and I knew it would take some of the edge off all my worries. I was soon to be twenty-nine, so I was most likely feeling the pressure of turning over another decade as well.

My parents were in a good place and I was happy for them. My father had climbed the corporate ladder and they had relocated to southern Indiana. My dad was a runner as well, and he had qualified for the Boston Marathon. They were traveling a great deal themselves, and I was happy they were enjoying their lives. I also felt more at ease about my pending exodus. I knew they were living a life of their own and would not feel devastated with Sofia and me far away.

Carlo and I booked a May trip to Florida to attend my Uncle Matt's wedding—and to celebrate Sofia's fourth birthday at Disney World. While we made plans, I waited anxiously to hear from Ireland. I was even more apprehensive about Sofia's father. Sofia still saw her paternal grandmother from time to time, but I no longer trusted the woman. I hated the moments when my anger boiled over. John had never spent a day with our baby— yet he had "paternal rights" that could dictate my life and hers! I resented the idea that he could interfere with my happiness. Obviously, I knew what was best for our daughter and had been her only real parent. I wanted him gone from our lives so badly—I didn't want his negative energy coming anywhere near my happy, perfect world. Thankfully, I had Pamela to vent to. She kept me sane as I sweated a possible, costly custody battle that could keep me from moving to Ireland. At least Sofia was young enough I didn't have to create any carefully-worded explanations—yet. I just tried to breathe and think positive thoughts as best I could.

One day, during lunch hour, I was seated in my cubicle and I decided to check my email. I caught my breath when I saw a transmission from University College Dublin. When I clicked it open and read the first few lines, my first impulse was to scream. I kept my composure, though, and with trembling hands I forwarded the email to Carlo with a heading that read, *Look, Baby! It's official!* I had been accepted into their MBS program!

Five minutes later, I phoned an attorney...

#

Easter of 2009 was glorious! It was the first Easter holiday I had spent with Sofia. Usually, I worked at the restaurant that day, as the money was great. I was delirious with happiness and anticipation of the coming changes in my life. Sofia and I traveled to my parents' home in Indiana. We went to church and had one of my mother's fabulous dinners. The yellow daffodils and fragrant hyacinths swayed in the breeze along the roadsides. Along with the budding trees, they were harbingers of my renewed life.

The chatter between Carlo and me was incessant. We discussed everything from closet space to day care (*creches*, in Ireland). Carlo was trying to find a larger house to accommodate the three of us and would send me photos of charming Irish houses that were located near parks.

April seventeenth was my twenty-ninth birthday. Carlo was flying in on a connecting flight from Chicago. Well, that was the plan, anyway. He phoned me at work to say that his flight to Chicago had been delayed four hours, which meant he'd miss his connection and would arrive a day later. Carlo's visit was only for a long weekend and I wasn't about to lose one precious day, so...

Around four that afternoon, when I clocked out for the day, Sofia and I hopped in my car and headed for Chicago. I had borrowed a friend's GPS for the trip. When we arrived in greater Chicago, it was nine o'clock at night and there were many detours due to construction. I became disoriented and started to panic. All at once I was driving on dark streets somewhere on the south side of town. Sofia began to complain that she had to pee. I didn't see a gas station or fast food place anywhere. "Baby," I said in desperation, "Mommy can't stop right now. You're going to have to pee in your car seat. I'm so sorry, honey, but that's our only option right now."

Sofia complained, of course. Who wouldn't? I was petrified in the meantime as I tried to get my bearings. By the time I found my way to O'Hare and saw Carlo walking straight for me at Arrivals, I was frazzled. I jumped out of my car and let him hold me for the longest time.

After a fourteen-hour round trip, we arrived back at my duplex at six in the morning. We all lay down to rest for a while after our mutual ordeals. Three hours later, I was awakened with a kiss and a "Happy Birthday". We eased into the morning with lots of cuddles and Sofia singing "Happy Birthday" to me in her adorable little voice. Then, Carlo said, "Go sit on the sofa and count to twenty." *Ok*.

I heard Carlo leave the room and return. Seconds later, he said, "Ok, open your eyes." Before me was a gorgeous, tan leather BRIC'S suitcase— the women's style that matched Carlo's. I couldn't wait to use it on our trip to Florida. He also gave Sofia a small bag, which she loved. Sofia was affectionately known as the "bag lady" as she had already amassed quite a collection.

Later, we took Sofia to spend the night at her cousin's house. Carlo and I decided to just hang out at my place and discuss our future. As we drove through downtown Dayton, we saw something I'll never forget: a voluptuous woman wearing some rather tiny shorts was standing on the street. We were stopped at a red light and I watched as she gripped both sides of a trash can and began "dirty dancing" for the passersby. Every body part was moving: it was a sight to see. I nudged Carlo, who looked over. "Did you bring me down here just for the show?" he asked casually. "Thank you so much for this unique experience!" We laughed so hard.

We did take a brief trip to Yellow Springs, our favorite Bohemian hang-out. We bought Sardinian wine, then headed for the grocery store to buy lobster, asparagus, and fresh tomatoes. Carlo made me a succulent birthday feast that night—I was impressed with his culinary skills.

The next day we picked up Sofia and met the family for further birthday revelry. The day after that was Sofia's indoor waterpark excursion, and then it was time for Carlo to leave for Ireland once more. This was the easiest goodbye yet, as I'd be seeing him in just a few weeks for our trip to my uncle's Florida wedding.

After Carlo left, I told Baca about my Ireland plans. She wasn't exactly thrilled—skeptical was more like. I told her I had contacted an attorney about her grandson's possible paternity suit. She asked a lot of questions. I think she was happy for me, but still taken aback by how quickly my life had changed and at the thought of Sofia and I being in a faraway land.

I wasn't insensitive to the perceptions of my rooted, Midwestern family as to my overwhelming and drastic life changes. I know it all seemed so odd to people who rarely left their own state that I would want to leave the good ol' US of A. Such is the way of people, sometimes, that they don't realize there is a whole world of people out there living equally as comfortable (and sometimes more so) and happy in a place they too call "home". In the end, my family expressed their happiness for me, because they knew it was the right thing to do.

I was so excited for our Florida trip that I didn't pack the most efficiently. By the time I landed I had two suitcases, a car seat, a sleeping Sofia and my carry-on. Thank goodness a kind stranger saw me struggling at baggage claim and assisted me while we located Carlo.

We attended the wedding in St. Pete Beach where Carlo met more of my family and then headed off for Miami to meet up with Pamela and our old friend, Andres. Andres' aunt kept Sofia while we went out that evening to celebrate Pam's birthday.

We celebrated Sofia's fourth birthday at Disney World, where she especially loved all the characters. I myself enjoyed the trip to fantasyland as well. It took me away from what awaited me back in Ohio: lawyers, paperwork, and stress...

"May the Road Rise Up..."

Journal: Tuesday, June 16, 2009

I am getting so excited for the move. Carlo, UCD, Ireland! Who would have ever known I would be going to graduate school in Ireland? I am living a Dream! ...57 days and counting! I got my hair cut the shortest it has ever been. I guess with such a big change I wanted to feel change on my person as well. I love my short hair!

After our Florida trip I had a lot of preparations to make. I met with my lawyer first thing, telling him the whole history of my ex, his estrangement, non-payment of support, all of it. He reassured me that he thought I was in a good position to relocate to Ireland for grad school. This made me breathe somewhat easier.

I also had to acquire a passport for Sofia—when I began to fill out the application, it required both parents' signatures! I panicked again, but my lawyer helped me draft a letter explaining my situation, and when Sofia's passport arrived in the mail some weeks later, I was elated.

Moving to another country is total upheaval. I had to sell everything I owned. Thankfully I was able to do that efficiently. My brother bought my car and friends and family bought my other personal items. So far, so good.

Target date for the move was August fifteenth. Carlo and I purchased three one-way tickets: he was flying over to take us back. In the meantime, he had found a house, was touring creches, and even decorating Sofia's new room! *Seriously, how did I find this guy?*

Sofia and I spent the balance of the summer saying goodbye to friends and family. She was accepting our big change with remarkable bravery. Of course, I didn't know how she would react when she wouldn't see her grandparents so regularly, but I could see my little girl was developing a very strong and independent character. I tried to nurture that strong will, without letting it get out of hand, of course. She also possessed a remarkably precocious sense of humor, which kept me entertained whenever we were together.

I also had to say goodbye to my job, my wonderful co-workers, and my clients. In my final days with social services, I encouraged my clients to set their goals and work toward them. I reminded them that I had once been in their shoes. Everyone makes their own futures, their own magic. I was a believer.

Finally, the final hurdle came: the August third hearing with Sofia's father. I asked my dad to go with me—I was a nervous wreck. Fate was in the balance: I visualized boarding the plane to Ireland with Carlo and Sofia, trying my best to will my future to fruition. When my ex and his current wife entered the courtroom, every muscle in my body tensed.

My attorney walked up and asked if I wanted to engage in some preliminary negotiations with my ex before the hearing started. I was more than willing. I was escorted into a small room and my ex and his wife soon joined us around the conference table.

My ex was in an apparent good mood. He looked at me, smiled, and said, "I'm not trying to be a dick! I'm here to tell the judge I'm ok with you taking her." After I exhaled, I couldn't ignore an underlying feeling of sadness for Sofia. This man hadn't seen her for four years, and even now, he didn't ask how she was. At least he wasn't being a complete egocentric jerk about the whole thing.

My ex further informed us that he was willing to give up all paternal rights to Sofia. I myself was willing to withdraw all demands for child support, both the back support ($11,000.00) that was owed, along with future payments.

During the hearing, the judge was agreeable to everything except the back support—my ex still had to pay it—and the relinquishment of paternal rights. The judge stated that, unless I had someone ready to adopt Sofia, that my ex would retain his rights as a father. When it was all said and done, though, Sofia and I were going to Ireland! Nothing else mattered. Jubilant, I left the courthouse looking into my future with anticipation.

In early August I had one final garage sale and began packing the basics. Carlo arrived in Ohio to help us tie up the final loose ends. I turned over the keys to my duplex to Rita and my car to my brother. We used my dad's pick-up to get around those last few days.

My folks had a small going-away party for Sofia and me. On the day of our departure, my parents drove us to Chicago to meet our flight. We had several hours in the car together that were accentuated by long silences. I know my parents were taking it hard, though they were happy for us.

When we arrived at O'Hare after a final meal together, my parents and Sofia had a tearful goodbye. It wasn't exactly easy for me, either. Poor Carlo must have felt like he was kidnapping the two of us. We made the usual promises and assurances to call, Skype, etcetera. We would be a click away at any moment of course—but it's still different knowing you can't just hop in the car and go have a meal with the people who love you.

My beautiful girl, my oh-so-special Carlo and yours truly landed in Dublin at six in the morning on August sixteenth 2009. The sun peeked over the horizon, heralding another dawn on the Emerald Isle, as the road to our future rose to greet us...

Home, in a Roundabout Way

C arlo had found a comfortable townhome in a suburb called Rath-farnham, an area surrounded by beautiful green mountains. Our place was in a development that was newer construction, not like the older, weathered historic row houses I had seen in Dublin.

When we walked in, I was taken with our quaint, furnished new home with its small, cozy rooms and back garden. The living room had a gas fireplace. Sofia's room was called a "box room". It barely fit a bed and a couple of toys, but Carlo had it decorated so cute for her. Every room was separate, with its own door—no open concept. The tight layout and odd appliances were something I had to get used to, but I was ready for our Irish adventure with the two most important people in my life. We spent the day getting over jetlag and getting acclimated. Carlo had taken some time off to help me adjust.

On our first morning in Dublin, Pamela's Uncle Kevin took us to The Goat near Goatstown, South Dublin, for a real Irish breakfast experience. I tried both white and black pudding for the first time. White pudding consists of oatmeal, pork, and spices and is formed to make a sausage. Black pudding is the same, only with blood added for flavor and color.

I contacted Pamela for a list of "must haves". She insisted on Brennan's bread, butter, and tea, among other items. This meant I'd have to learn to drive myself to the grocery—easier said than done.

My first driving lesson with Carlo was in a 2003 Renault with manual transmission. Sitting on the "wrong" side of the car, driving on the "wrong" side of the road, and navigating narrow roads and three-lane roundabouts was a terrifying experience. I felt as if I were driving a car for the first time.

Carlo first took me on back roads to get me comfortable with the car and driving on the left side of the road. I wanted to stay on back roads, but in time we approached a three-lane roundabout where cars were circling at what I would have called "NASCAR speed". I had Carlo in my peripheral vision as my knuckles turned white on the wheel. He was smirking in amusement, quietly challenging me to get over my fear.

I entered the roundabout and drove around the circle several times before he told me to get off at the third exit. "I wanted you to understand," he said, "that if you get confused you can keep driving around the circle until you decide what you will do next."

A day or two later, my first trip to the grocery was a learning experience. I put Sofia in her car seat and drove the two blocks to Tesco. It was difficult parking in the little narrow space on an incline. Then, I discovered that I had to pay one euro for a "buggy" or cart. I dug a euro out of the bottom of my purse and Sofia and I went inside and followed the other shoppers.

I found some things on my list, but other things were not so easy. I asked a clerk for things that he had never heard of. There was no "mac and cheese". Eggs were on a shelf next to the bread. "Courgettes" turned out to be zucchini.

When I got to the checkout, I had to "bag" my own groceries. People were staring at me, apparently taken aback by all the items I had purchased. I felt awkward as I tried to quickly pack my purchases. Finally, I paid the clerk my euros and Sofia and I made our way to the parking lot. The wheels on the buggy were multi-directional, so pushing the heavy cart uphill was challenging. The buggy kept sliding in all directions as cold rain fell all around us. I was relieved to finally get to my car. When we got home, I realized my small Irish fridge was not going to accommodate my American-sized shopping list. I had to push, shove, wiggle, and cram to get the door to close. I just hoped when I opened it the stuff wouldn't come flying out onto the floor!

Carlo had to return to work and Sofia and I were on our own. I still had some time before my classes began and Sofia would go to her creche. We made a routine of walking to Rathfarnham Castle Park. It was a ten-minute walk down a narrow street, past the Yellow House Pub and a large cathedral, the "Church of the Annunciation".

On our first trip to the park, the wind was brisk. Sofia and I donned sweatshirts and sweatpants. When we arrived at the park and saw all the Irish mums, I was chagrined to find that I had under-dressed for the occasion. I didn't understand that I was living in a "posh" area of Dublin. The ladies were in dressy clothes, with polished boots. I might as well have worn my pajamas. From then on, I left my Dayton, Ohio playground dress code behind.

I was thrilled to discover we had American neighbors next door. Peter and Kelly were a couple with three young children. They had lived in Ireland for five years—Peter's grandparents were Irish. He was a history professor at a local college and Kelly had a degree in archeology but was a stay-at-home mom. She loved animals—they had several dogs and cats. After we met, Kelly became a dog-walker. One sight I will never forget is the first time I saw Peter pushing the pram and reading a book while he walked to get groceries—he was quite the multi-tasker.

Kelly was so helpful and kind. She taught me a great deal about the culture and gave me tools for survival. I learned new words for things and discovered that there was a "TV tax". I learned that at a certain time of day the post office was "Closed for Tea". I continued my routine of reading. Sofia and I made lots of trips to the library and I delved into Irish authors.

One thing I struggled with was the climate. Our home always felt cold—Carlo told me I needed to wear layers. I often hovered near the radiator. It was difficult coming from a place where you had definitive seasons and central heat.

I never ventured far from our neighborhood, but Sofia and I took trips to nearby stores, the park, and I showed her the creche where she would soon go. I was mobile enough to not feel isolated or stranded.

Carlo drove me to my first day at UCD Smurfit School of Business. As we drove onto the motorway and I looked out at the green hills, I asked myself again, *How did I get here?* I quickly made friends with two Irish girls who were in the same program, which consisted of about thirty students. I was ready to immerse myself in my studies.

I was in class three days a week for four hours. Friday was my study day—and that was special. I chose the converted attic above Carlo's office for my quiet spot. It was comforting knowing he was at the foot of the stairs while I pored over my notes.

I had a project management assignment that was a group project. My project group looked like the United Nations: Irish, American, Brazilian, Italian, and South Korean. The topic we chose was fitting: issues that a project manager faces when overseeing a diverse team in a foreign country. We selected Carlo's company for our case study! Carlo led a team from Ireland, Poland, Italy, and Slovakia. It's probably no surprise that we got the top grade in the class.

In those first few months, the three of us were slowly becoming a family. Sofia bonded with Carlo and his influence on her was positive. There were some ups and downs, but nothing out of the ordinary. I had some occasional bouts of homesickness, but not to the point that I was miserable. We gradually developed a comfortable routine that suited all our tastes. Sofia's favorite restaurant was Johnny Fox's Pub. Situated in Glencullen in the mountains above Dublin, it's considered one of the oldest and most traditional Irish pubs. There was live music nightly, great food, and their famous "Hooley Night"—dinner and Irish dance. It became our go-to spot for whenever we had visitors. Sofia would often put on her best party dress and come downstairs, regally announcing that she was "ready to go to Johnny Fox's". We would usually take her up on her spontaneity. Carlo and I enjoyed it as well.

The three of us took our first trip to Sardinia within a couple of months of arriving in Ireland. I was so excited for Sofia to experience what I had only one year before. It was a quick getaway, but a nice break from school for me. Sofia loved Carlo's parents and Selli. She also loved the beach, the language, the food, and the shopping. My little girl was becoming quite sophisticated for not even being in elementary school yet.

When Christmas rolled around, we planned back-to-back trips to Sardinia and the US. It was the usual holiday runaround of lost luggage, delayed or cancelled flights, and of course a four-year-old. We were in Dublin, Rome, Cagliari, Chicago, Indianapolis, and Columbus all in one two-week holiday! I must say that I appreciated the less hectic, less commercial way in which Sardinians celebrated: the time was about good food and togetherness, not so much about presents. I loved Vittoria's home-cooked meals over the fireplace, her Christmas tree, and her nativity scene. She taught me to make pizza during our visit.

These trips were packed to the max with activity—we were exhausted when we returned home—but every moment with our loved ones was joyful. Could I possibly have any *more* joy? *Hmmmm...*

"A Little Boy with Hearts in his Eyes"

One night before bed, I was taking off my make-up. I looked up to find Carlo watching me in the mirror. "I look like a little boy with hearts in my eyes," he said. "I wonder if I always look like this when I look at you."

What could I possibly do but melt?

Our relationship continued to grow stronger. I looked forward to each day I spent with my handsome Italian and my beautiful girl. We were a tightly-knit trio, too: we acted like tourists, taking excursions to Irish castles, parks, cities, and festivals.

In March, I attended the UCD Michael Smurfit ball—it had an Oscars theme and was held at an old castle in the countryside. I purchased a black ball gown and other accessories for the fancy affair. All Master's students were invited to the event, but when I asked my female colleagues if they were bringing their "significant others", they looked at me like I was crazy. "It would just be awkward," they said, "for us to have them tagging along. They don't know anyone—it will be more fun hanging out with our friends!"

Well…

If this was the way they raised women in Ireland, I must say, I liked it. After a few drinks, the band played "Galway Girl" and I joined in and danced as if I'd been born in Galway myself. I had a fun and memorable evening.

#

Journal: Sunday, February 28, 2010

Today I am pretty excited! Carlo, Sofia and I are going on a road trip across Ireland, France, Switzerland and Italy. Our plan is to drive to the south of Ireland, take an overnight ferry to France, spend a few days in Paris, drive through the alps to Genoa, take another overnight ferry to Sardinia and spend the remaining days there and fly back to Dublin. This adventure will be an experience of a lifetime!

When we arrived at Cherbourg, France on the ferry, the first thing I noticed was Carlo speaking French to the port guards. I had no idea he had this hidden talent. I loved his confidence and his ability to take things head-on. We arrived in Paris at seven that evening and checked in to our fifth-floor studio apartment where we would be staying for the next few days. We dropped our luggage, grabbed a taxi and headed straight for the Eiffel Tower!

Sofia's first taxi ride was quite an experience—for Mommy, that is. I closed my eyes as our driver sped through traffic, hard-braking and weaving between cars. I sat back and closed my eyes, trying to relax. The three of us were eating crepes at the foot of the Tower in no time. We also went to the Champs-Élysées and walked through the Arc de Triomphe.

After a good night's sleep and more sumptuous crepes, we further explored the "City of Lights". The Louvre, Notre Dame, the parks, statues, and bridges—it was all so breathtaking. I had never seen so much art and architecture in one place. Sofia had fallen asleep by the time we reached Notre Dame. Carlo carried her on his shoulder for the better part of the afternoon. That evening, we took a romantic walk along the Seine and had dinner at a little restaurant on a side street. Carlo ordered escargot. I wanted to try it once more, but the snails' eyes looking at me was a bit too much.

The next morning, we hopped in our car and drove through the French countryside—Provence. I looked out at breathtaking castles, rolling hills, vineyards, and quaint villages. Soon, we arrived at the Alps: more castles, tunnels, and towering, snow-capped mountains.

We stopped at a small Italian restaurant in Courmayeur, not far from the famous Mont Blanc. I had the most divine tiramisu and cappuccino. Then, it was off to Genoa to board the ferry for the last leg of our trip.

The next day we arrived in Sardinia. We drove straight to Stintino, where we grabbed breakfast, walked along the Mediterranean, had some beach time, and enjoyed a pizza in Alghero.

On the tail end of our trip, we drove to Cagliari to see the Pilia family. Vittoria and I bonded further on this trip. She told me, in Italian, "My family is my life, and you are a part of it."

We spent our remaining vacation enjoying the Sardinian sunshine, the beautiful beaches, fantastic food and time with the family. Vittoria never ceased to inspire me. She was a woman who truly put her family first. I would look at her and then look at my amazing Carlo, her sweet, loving, thoughtful boy: this time, I had hearts in *my* eyes.

Plans...

In March, not long after we returned from our tour of Europe, my parents arrived. I was so excited to show them my new home. It was their first trip to Europe and I wanted to make it memorable. I tried to immerse them in the culture and show them that I was happy and living a full life. It was fun to see their reactions to a new country. They were especially shocked to see the Irish swimming in the sea at that time of year. My parents were bundled up in gloves and scarves. We took them to our favorite restaurants, toured castles, and did a lot of hiking and sight-seeing. They left shortly before my thirtieth birthday.

For my birthday, Carlo had scheduled an overnight getaway to a countryside castle. I pushed back, saying that I wanted to be home for when my Uncle Matt and his wife Carina arrived. They were scheduled to fly in the day after my birthday. Carlo urged me to go, saying that things would be fine, but I insisted.

So, the evening of my birthday we went to Dundrum Town Centre and had cocktails at Harvey Nichols and dinner at Siam Thai. We enjoyed some live entertainment and had a fun evening. When we arrived home, Carlo said, "I still need to give you your present. Go upstairs and I'll call you down when I am ready."

I complied. After all, it wasn't the first time he had surprised me. A few minutes later, Carlo called for me and I came downstairs. He had lit the fireplace, and there were candles glowing. He told me to sit down and close my eyes. I took a seat in a chair, closed my eyes and waited.

On cue, I opened my eyes and Carlo was kneeling before me, holding a ring. "Do you want to marry me?" he asked.

I was bubbling over with happiness. Somewhere in all my ecstasy I thought that I uttered the word "Yes", but Carlo insists to this day that all I did was smile and look deep into his eyes. We held each other for the longest time. It was a good thing, too—without Carlo's arms around me I most certainly would have floated to the moon. I couldn't wait to tell our families, Pamela, and our other friends. How nice that we'd be able to share our happiness with Uncle Matt and Aunt Carina—I thought it rather serendipitous, since we had just been at their wedding not long ago, and they were the first of my family to meet Carlo, on our romantic first weekend in New York City…

Things don't always go according to plan—just ask my poor Carlo. First, my aunt and uncle did not arrive. Volcanic ash from Iceland had forced the cancellation of their trans-Atlantic flight. Carlo revealed to me that he had planned the castle getaway in order to set the romantic mood for his proposal. I could have kicked myself for not going—but I was still the happiest woman on the planet.

When we called my parents to tell them the news, they had a story for me:

"Remember back when we were in Ireland and we were all in the restaurant in Bray?" my mother asked. "When you left the table to take Sofia to the bathroom, Carlo asked us for your hand in marriage."

"I looked over at your mother. Tears were streaming down her face. I was crying as well. We were both so happy."

Carlo told me that after Sofia and I returned to the table, they all were straining to pretend that nothing had happened.

I had to laugh off my thwarting Carlo's "big moment", but, in the end, what better place to receive a proposal of marriage than in the home you've already made with your best friend? I admit, though, I've since learned to "go with the flow", as you never know when you'll be surprised.

#

That summer, Sofia and I traveled to the US for my Aunt Emily's wedding. Sofia was a flower girl. This put me in the mood to go shopping for my own wedding dress, and Pamela accompanied me on my search. I found the perfect dress after nine hours of shopping: a form-fitting, strapless, white satin and tulle dress with a black sash. I couldn't wait for our wedding day...

I was quickly approaching the end of my master's program as well. All the studying, projects, and papers were taking their toll. The final exam process at Smurfit was totally foreign to me. The exams were held in a huge hall, where we sat in rows of at least fifty people while moderators walked up and down the aisles. It reminded me of taking my SAT. We were required to write an essay and we had no idea what the question would be. I struggled with knowing how to study for such a subjective test and relied on my Irish girlfriends for help with studying tips.

I was also trying to plan a wedding while attending to all my other daily responsibilities as a parent. I was becoming a little frazzled.

Carlo sensed I needed an evening out and we got dressed up and attended the Engineers of Ireland 175th Anniversary concert. What a musical feast—a Celtic harp orchestra, dancing, bagpipes, and the Irish Army band. People broke out in song at the end of the evening. One wouldn't think an engineers ball would be all that exciting, but the Irish know how to celebrate in style no matter the occasion or profession.

My class decided to organize a final soiree or last outing before we all graduated. I was reluctant, with all my wedding plans and other things on my mind. Carlo nudged me to go, telling me he and Sofia would enjoy their evening together and that I would "regret it" if I didn't spend that final night with my class. Let's just say that Laurie doesn't make the same mistake twice. I listened to Carlo and on that night he dropped me off at the party location.

When I entered the building, I got the shock of my life: all thirty of my classmates had organized a "hen party", otherwise known as a "bachelorette party". The best part of the evening was playing a game called "How Well Do You Know Carlo?" I was in the hotseat while my friends fired questions about my fiancé (They had interviewed him previously for the occasion). I must admit I got nearly all thirty correct.

My dearest old friend Abigail, who had attended Sofia's birth, had insisted on being my wedding planner. She had been there since the beginning—it was only fitting that she helped orchestrate my big day. She volunteered to be the photographer, to make the cake, design jewelry, and arrange flowers. How lucky I was to have her!

The first item on the list was to choose a location. Carlo and I revisited the Irish castle idea, but getting married in Ireland meant I'd have to convert to Catholicism. The cold and rainy climate was also a concern. We wanted some guarantee of sunshine to light up one of the brightest days of our lives.

We needed a date and a sunny, mid-way point for Carlo's and my families: August 20th in Barbados. It would be a ten-day event, and Carlo booked a six-bedroom villa for family and guests. He also booked flights for the family and made various other arrangements.

The plans were set, and I started yet another countdown on my calendar...

Bella Barbados

Two days after turning in my final essays for my master's—about 40,000 words—Carlo, Sofia, and I left for Barbados and our island fantasy wedding. After connecting with Carlo's family in London, we flew to Barbados together and landed in Bridgetown on August sixteenth. A gentleman named Tyrone met us at the airport and drove us to our villa.

As we made the hour drive along the gently sloping, terraced plains that bordered the coast, various islanders waved in greeting. It was surreal. We arrived at the Sea Symphony Villa and were greeted by the staff, including our personal chef, Margaret. The villa had a breathtaking view of the Caribbean and a private pool. Carlo's family, Sofia, and I were lounging by the pool when my parents arrived later that day.

The first order of business was to meet the pastor and obtain our marriage license. After our meeting with clergy, my father drove Carlo and me back to Bridgetown to take care of the official details. We obtained our "stamp" at the Post Office and then went to the local registrar to sign the final documents.

After the paperwork was finished, we asked a local woman on the street to recommend a place for lunch.

"Follow me," she said.

The three of us followed her to a tiny shopping mall. We took an escalator to the second-floor book shop, passed through a women's department and the next thing we knew we were walking through a tiny door into a small, buffet-style restaurant. We were the only tourists in the place, and we had an authentic, Barbadian dining experience. I highly recommend the famous "flying fish" and "macaroni pie".

The next day we took a pontoon boat excursion with our family and friends, taking in the breathtaking view of the blue waters, snorkeling near a shipwreck, and looking at various aquatic life. The high point was swimming with sea turtles.

Abigail, Pamela, and Giosue, Carlo's best man, arrived two days before the wedding. Correction: Giosue was *supposed* to have arrived. He was flying in from Peru. We waited around the airport after we connected with Abigail and Pamela—no Giosue. Carlo was unfazed. He knew his unpredictable, globe-trotting friend well. We drove back to the villa in hopes that our best man would find us. Our cell phones did not work in Barbados.

The following day we had to handle the floral arrangements. We visited a small flower shop and chose an assortment of lilies, baby's breath, and peach-colored roses. There was lots of running around, and things weren't without some re-grouping. Upon our arrival, we had to be directed to a new pastor as our original was in recovery from a recent heart attack. Then, we had to rent a second house last minute, as things got a bit crowded with twenty-three guests. Thank goodness my mother was there to entertain Sofia. She was happy to spend time with her little granddaughter, whom she missed.

One of my most vivid memories during all the preparations was Pamela rescuing a cow. Yes, a cow. We were in the car on some errand and she looked out the window and saw a cow tied to a tree. The bovine had become tangled in its rope and was in distress. It was Pamela to the rescue. My dear friend, always at the right place at the right time for everyone, people and cows alike.

I must admit, my fiancé was stressed. He was trying to handle so much, please everyone, and be a translator. I did depend on him a lot.

Even with my recent travels, I was still a small-town Ohioan and he was more worldly. It was the first and only time I ever witnessed Carlo being overwhelmed. Of course, it was a momentous day in his life as well. It was taxing to attend to everyone's needs while trying to enjoy his own wedding celebration. I reassured him he could relax more and that everything would be fine. In the end, he rose to every occasion. I can say without a doubt that my loyal, sensitive Italian would make a fine ambassador to the United Nations!

The night before the wedding, Carlo was in the pool when he saw a familiar silhouette against the sunset. Giosue had arrived! When we later pressed him for how he had found us, he replied that he simply asked around at the airport and someone thought they knew where he needed to go. Amazing. Our wedding party was now complete.

One of the funniest moments happened at dinner the night before the wedding. Vittoria produced a letter that Carlo had written at eighteen. It said, "If I ever want to get married, please kick my ASS!" Carlo had said he would never get married and Vittoria bet him that someday he would change his mind. She promptly walked over and gave him a swift kick in his posterior.

Miracle-worker Abigail produced her bakery bag of tricks and began constructing our wedding cake. Last minute preparations were being made. Everyone was lending a hand wherever they could. Sofia was excited to wear her dress that matched mine.

The day of the wedding, my hairdresser, Donna, arrived and we began to turn me into the bride that my Carlo deserved. Abigail photographed the process of my transformation: at one point, she paused and looked at me. With tears in her eyes, she said, "You look so beautiful". Both of us had years of friendship flash before our eyes. Could either of us have predicted this a mere five years ago?

That afternoon, at five o'clock, in the most magical island setting I could imagine, I promised my life to Carlo, forever. My teary-eyed father walked me to the flower-festooned gazebo, whispering how happy he was for us. When he handed me off to my future husband, I immersed myself in Carlo's amber eyes as we said our vows—well, sort of said. The minister's thick Barbadian accent was a little too much for Carlo. He wasn't sure what to repeat after he said, "Repeat after me." He mumbled his way through, figuring only I would hear him and that the minister would simply think he was speaking in his Italian accent.

It didn't matter anyway. All we saw was each other's reflections in our eyes, and a bright and welcoming horizon beyond. My little Sofia was our flower girl. She stood there in that little gazebo, alongside Carlo and me. My precious daughter and I had found our prince: we welcomed him with open, grateful, and loving hearts. *Ti amo moltissimo....*

That evening, as the sun set over aquamarine waters, we had a marvelous party at the villa. Pamela, my Irish "fairy godmother" who made my whole Cinderella fantasy happen, was there at the grand ball of my lifetime, dancing Celtic dances with Sofia. Everyone ate, drank, danced, and made merry. Carlo let off a little steam and tossed his unsuspecting father into the pool while he still wore his white dress shirt. The next thing I knew, in solidarity with Daniele, *everyone was in the pool!* The men jumped in wearing their white dress shirts, and the women wore bathing suits but grabbed white shirts and put them over them. It was quite a scene!

Carlo and I left for our honeymoon. We drove to the south side of Barbados and stayed at the Almond Casuarina resort. We had a relaxing time together, enjoying the beach and the nightlife—mostly just celebrating our Irish luck at having found each other. We reflected on that first day in Pamela's uncle's "carpark"—and all the crazy magic that had happened since. It had been quite a journey, from Dublin to Dayton, from Sardinia to Chicago, and a few points in between. We slept on cool linens, wrapped in each other's arms, and dreamt of adventures yet to unfold.

Erin Go *What?*

After our fantasy in Barbados, it was back home to Dublin. We had another big change on our horizon: Sofia was starting school! Now that I had finished my master's degree, I also needed to find a job. In the meantime, I helped out at Carlo's office while Sofia was at school. I also began to aggressively study Italian. I wanted to communicate with my new family.

We enrolled Sofia in the junior infant class at Loreto Grange Road. The all-girls school was located behind the former abbey of the same name and was founded by Mother Frances Teresa Ball in 1823. It is the school where little Anjexë Gonxhe Bojaxhiu, now known as St. Teresa of Calcutta or "Mother Teresa", began her studies. I was anxious that Sofia like her school.

My daughter was way more ready than I was. She looked so grown-up in her green plaid pinafore and blue jumper (sweater). I loved the uniform routine—it made life so easy when getting ready in the morning. I had less laundry to do as well. The girls always wore their hair tied back, and no nail "varnish"! A healthy lunch policy limited treats to Fridays. We enrolled her in ballet and Irish dance.

In the mornings, Sofia would hop on her scooter and I would run alongside her as we traveled the half-mile or so to the school. In the afternoon, the mums and dads would line up outside the gate, awaiting dismissal. Sofia's new parochial school adventure added a new dimension to my life—my social life, that is. I enjoyed getting to know the other mothers as we waited for our children outside the school gate. It seemed that we were sending Sofia off to a birthday party every weekend.

My big challenge was Sofia's Irish language homework. I had no experience with this compulsory area of study. I was having enough trouble with Italian! The first phrase small children learn is, "*An bhfuil cead agam dul amach go dtí an leithreas?*" which means "May I be excused to the toilet?" Sofia learned songs, words, poems, and phrases. Being so little, her brain easily absorbed the language much better than I.

I became a part of a group of Irish mums and finally had a social life of my own. I had had good times with my classmates, but they were all five to seven years younger than I, and single. The mums and I had much more in common. I made new friends—Kathy, Isabell, Shaheena, and Eavan. These women were from different parts of the world and became important, permanent facets of my life. Not only did we organize play dates with our kids, but we also organized "playdates" of our own. This included organizing fundraisers—one where we hiked twenty miles across the Irish hills—having teas, going shopping, attending various events and festivals, taking trips to seaside towns, and of course, "Mums' Night Out". We had "great *craic*" as the Irish say. My friendships with these women enriched my life and my knowledge in an incomparable way. They made my last year in Ireland something to be cherished.

#

That year was the first and only Christmas I didn't spend with my parents. We decided to spend Christmas at home in Rathfarnham. We purchased a real tree and hiked the hills gathering pinecones and greenery. I will never forget Sofia waking up on Christmas morning and saying in her Irish brogue: "Rudolph ate the carrot."

We opened presents and then had a traditional Irish breakfast of bacon rashers, pork sausages, fried or scrambled eggs, white pudding, black pudding, toast, fried tomato, sautéed field mushrooms, baked beans, hash browns, and soda bread. We were quickly becoming Irish!

My mom arrived shortly after Christmas and offered to keep Sofia while Carlo and I went on a little getaway—to Galway. The harbor city's hub is 18th century Eyre Square, with its shops, pubs, and traditional Irish music. One day we drove to see the Cliffs of Moher. We were bundled from head to toe as we got out of the car, took in the majestic 700ft cliffs that towered over the Atlantic, snapped a photo and then ran into the little museum to get warm!

As 2011 dawned, Carlo and I had to begin the process of more major decision-making. I had started a new, temporary job at a communications firm in Dublin, on Grafton Street. I loved getting off the bus in the middle of the bustling city and going to work, but the job was for only six weeks, and in a struggling economy, Carlo and I had to look ahead.

We had always discussed the possibility of living in the States, but that meant Carlo would have to get a green card. I wasn't in a hurry to leave Ireland, necessarily. We had just begun to feel at home and settled, but we had to weigh the benefits of geography versus our economic future. It would also be advantageous for Sofia to be in closer proximity to at least one side of her family.

We began the arduous process of the paperwork, but soon found out that Carlo would need a sponsor. My parents assisted immediately. There were various screenings and even a physical examination, which caught my husband off guard. He had no idea they would scrutinize him so intimately.

In the middle of this planning, something unplanned occurred...

Clouds and Sunshine

Carlo and I were madly in love, and yet we weren't planning on having children right away. But we were so in love that we weren't doing anything to avoid more children, either. We figured whatever happened was just another result of our happiness.

So, when I discovered I was pregnant in the spring of 2011, I was pleasantly surprised, but not shocked. When I told Carlo he was excited, and we decided to tell our families right away, mostly because I was going to the US in just a few short weeks, and we didn't want to tell my folks without Carlo there. Everyone was happy for us, of course. I was ecstatic. I had a serenity about me I had never experienced before. I had been younger and less mature when I was pregnant with Sofia. I was still struggling to know myself. More importantly, I didn't have the dependable, stable, loving husband that I had now.

Sofia and I went to the States in April to see my parents. We were on our flight, somewhere over the Atlantic, when I suddenly felt some cramping. I went to the bathroom and discovered the worst: I was having a miscarriage. It was awful, being in a plane with my five-year-old daughter and no Carlo. I had to be strong for Sofia and not appear to be upset. I just hugged her as I quietly mourned the little spark of life that was leaving my body.

As soon as we landed, I informed my parents and phoned Carlo. He was sad over the baby of course but more worried about me. He wanted to fly over to be with us, but I told him there was no need. I was with my family and I would be ok. I saw my doctor in Ohio as soon as I could and the miscarriage was confirmed, though I hardly needed confirmation. I mourned our loss and hoped that we might get another chance.

There were further discussions about our moving back to the US. It made me sad to think about it. I had grown to love my Irish friends and my newfound culture. Then, in June, Carlo received his visa and we discovered we were limited to a six-month window to relocate. If we were going to do this, we had to start making plans immediately.

It was about this time that Carlo was invited to lunch at the Italian ambassador's villa in Lucan. The sun was shining as people dined in tents set up in the gardens. Huge platters, resplendent with enticing food, were served up as people mingled and got acquainted. Carlo and I visited with ambassadors from other countries. It was an amazing afternoon.

At one point, I heard an American accent. When you're in a foreign country, someone who "sounds like home" is suddenly like your long-lost cousin. We engaged this gentleman and ended up being invited to a Fourth of July celebration at the home of the American ambassador, the late Dan Rooney. I couldn't believe our luck!

We went and had a marvelous time. Sofia played in the bouncy house while Carlo and I drank Starbucks coffee and watched a football game. We met several other Americans and ate traditional Fourth of July fare: hotdogs, hamburgers, chips.

I continued to focus on being Sofia's mom and thinking ahead about our move. I also continued to study my Italian: Sofia and I were about to head to Sardinia for a long summer holiday. Carlo would be joining us for the last week of our visit, so I wouldn't have a translator the whole time. I was determined to communicate with my in-laws.

Sofia and I joined Daniele and Vittoria at their seaside house in Stintino. We enjoyed the beach, swimming in the turquoise water and playing in the sand. I went for a run frequently, taking in the sea air and gazing at the mountains in the distance. Being in this island paradise was a healing experience for me, after my miscarriage and all the stress of planning our move. My Italian improved immensely, as speaking English wasn't an option. We relied heavily on a translation book. Sofia learned some words as well while she ate lots of homemade pasta and pastries.

Three weeks later, Carlo arrived. I was so glad to have him close to me again. When we weren't spending time with his family, we talked about the looming change. We decided to just enjoy the coming days until we left for America, treating them like an extended holiday. We wrote down our goals on a piece of paper, put it in a glass wine bottle and threw it out to sea, thinking that giving over control of our future to the whims of the currents would take away our stress. We would let the unpredictable waters take us where they may...

The Wind at Our Backs

After the three of us returned to Ireland from Sardinia, Abigail arrived for a month-long visit. I was so excited to have my dearest friend there with me. I loved showing her my new world. We hiked the hills, visited Malahide Castle, went out to the pubs—all the while Abigail had her camera at the ready to record some wonderful memories. We drove to the Indian grocery one evening and she cooked a fabulous Indian meal for us. In the last days of her stay, Sofia started Senior Infants at Loreto. Abigail got to experience the walk to school and waiting with the other mums in the schoolyard.

Carlo and I celebrated our one-year anniversary by going out on the town. Abigail obliged us by babysitting Sofia. After dinner at Wagamama, we watched Riverdance, which was phenomenal. Then, we took a walk down Memory Lane: we strolled over to the Russell Court Hotel, the place where "Carlo and Laurie" began, a mere three years before. We marveled at how much had happened in a short time.

We chose November nineteenth as our date of departure. Those last few months were spent living Irish life to the fullest, visiting our favorite places for the last time while we said farewell to friends. We took one last trip to Sardinia. We would no longer have the convenient, two-hour flight to visit Vittoria and Daniele. Sofia was excited to move closer to her family, but sad to leave her friends.

Carlo reached out to an American professor he knew and through this connection he garnered an interview in Manchester, England, with the prospect of working for an American company, the largest in his industry. Things went well and there was a promise to stay in touch. I was happy that Carlo was establishing some connections in the US.

The mums threw a going-away party for me at the Yellow House Pub. I was going to miss our *craic* and all the friendship. They had all come to mean so much to me.

When it came time to pack, my German friend Isabell helped me. She joked that she had a "license to pack"—a reference to her always telling me how Germany had a license for everything: riding a bike, swimming in a pool, etc. We packed fifteen suitcases and three carry-ons.

Isabell, Pam's Uncle Kevin and Carlo's co-worker Simone drove us to the airport. It wasn't easy managing all those suitcases. There were tearful goodbyes as we left the Emerald Isle. I had flown away from it almost four years before, a "green" young woman on a Celtic high after a wild weekend of partying in Temple Bar, thinking that I'd want to live there someday. "Someday" had come swiftly in the form of amber, Sardinian eyes and a love unexpected. I had truly *lived* in Ireland, on a much more fulfilling and wondrous adventure than I ever could have imagined. I had given my young daughter the experience of a lifetime, one that would define her as she grew into adulthood. Now, my Dublin Dream was coming to an end.

Carlo, Sofia, and I boarded our flight to America with heavy, hopeful hearts.

Back Home Again

W e settled in with my parents in the little town of Batesville, Indiana. Located about forty minutes from Cincinnati, it was settled by Germans in the early nineteenth century. The town is very blonde, consequently, as well as very neat and orderly. The original home of Hill-Rom Industries, a Fortune 500 company, the town enjoyed a certain standard of living that was rare for that area.

Of course, it was a far cry from Ireland, but we planned to be there only for a few months until we found jobs. The company Carlo had connected with in Manchester had headquarters in Clearwater, Florida and he planned to fly down for an interview.

Sofia had to immediately enroll in school. It was quite a change: public school, no uniforms, boys in her classroom, school lunch, and riding the "yellow school bus". We got a call from Sofia's teacher telling us that Sofia refused to ride the bus home, saying that she was used to a double-decker bus and that she didn't like "the smells on the American bus". Carlo and I drove my father's Ford pick-up to school to collect our fussy first grader. On the way home, she told us, "I did not get to eat my lunch because I sat next to a really good talker."

Carlo and I flew to Tampa so that he could meet with his prospective employers. I attended a job fair and did some shopping. While he got no immediate job offer, things looked promising.

Our stay in Florida was especially memorable as we stayed in Sarasota with my Grandpa and Grandma Evans, my mother's father and stepmother. My grandparents were retired scientists who had taught biochemistry research at UMASS. I loved our intellectual conversations and learning about my past.

Carlo and I returned to Batesville with hopes of living in sunny Florida, but we kept our options open. Meanwhile, life with my parents was fun: we took turns cooking family dinners and enjoying the wine from my dad's collection. We joined the local YMCA. I spent time in yoga classes and Sofia enrolled in gymnastics.

One day, Pamela came over from Columbus, about a two-hour drive, and my parents took us on a drive in the Indiana countryside. As we traveled along Indiana Highway 3, we came across a little hamlet called "Sardinia". We were so intrigued we had to stop. Pamela took Carlo's and my picture as we stood in front of the little sign at the side of the road. In the background were farms and cornfields—no turquoise water or anything reminiscent of Carlo's island home. I wondered to myself how the town had taken its name.

After obtaining drivers licenses, we went to Cincinnati and purchased a much-needed car, a 2004 Mercedes, thanks to Carlo's excellent negotiating skills.

When Carlo received the call with an offer from the company in Florida, we were ecstatic. He would be a Senior Project Manager with a six-figure salary. It was time to move again, but we were not fazed. It was just another adventure in the life of Carlo, Laurie, and Sofia. A bonus was that my brother Nicholas was going to join us. Carlo had suggested that he move with us, and to my surprise, he accepted the offer.

On Valentine's Day, 2012, we drove away from snowy Batesville, headed for Florida sunshine. Fourteen hours later, we arrived at our new apartment in Oviedo, a suburb of East Orlando. Exhausted, we slept on the floor with pillows and blankets. The rest of our belongings—our fifteen suitcases with our Irish acquisitions—would arrive on a moving truck the next day.

You Don't Have to
Shovel Sunshine

We awoke to a balmy, sunny Florida morning. As we sat outside a McDonald's, having breakfast and waiting for the moving truck, we pondered all the work we had to do to get settled. Of course, we had to buy virtually everything: furniture, linens, dishes, daily household items. It would be fun creating a new home, but after buying a car, the expenses were racking up. It would be a while before we recouped.

Our apartment complex felt like a resort: gym, pool, hot tub, game room. It was nice to have these amenities to work off stress as we started new jobs, looked for jobs, or, in Sofia's case, started yet another new school. In a slowly recovering economy, I was struggling to find an HR position since I had no experience. I decided to just focus on Sofia and getting our home together and wait until after the summer's end to resume my search.

Sofia and I had a wonderful, relaxing summer together. We hung out at the pool, made new friends, and explored our new Florida surroundings. It was nice to just spend time with my daughter after the years of working two jobs as a single mom and packing her off to daycare.

As soon as Sofia began second grade, I resumed my job search. I was contacted by a temp agency for a week-and-a-half assignment: it lasted a year and a half. I was getting the job experience I needed, Carlo was happy in his work, and Sofia was making new friends and taking karate after school. Life as we knew it was simple and we were happy.

#

Usually when a person hits their thirties they start thinking about life's finite reality. As people fill out life insurance forms at their jobs and privately, naming beneficiaries, etcetera, certain thoughts come to mind. Sometimes I would look at Sofia and see some little part of my ex, and I would think, "What happens to her if something happens to me?" The legal realities terrified me. I had given my daughter a wondrous and healthy life with loving people all around her. Specifically, I had placed a mentally healthy, responsible, and loving "father" in her life: Carlo. Yet, if something happened, her "next of kin" did not bode well for her future. I had no idea what my ex was doing. I only knew he would not provide for Sofia in the way that Carlo could and would. No more travel, no more culture, no more positive inspiration and concern for her well-rounded education. *What to do?*

One day I sat down with Carlo and asked him if he would be willing to adopt Sofia. He readily agreed to the idea. Any good man who loves a woman loves her children, too. They are her heart: he can't love one and not love the other.

I hired an attorney and she sent my ex a letter. He responded with a phone call. I had hoped that his good-natured attitude in the courtroom a few years ago would still prevail, but my Irish luck had dried up in the Floridian sun. He responded with a phone call, raving that I had taken his daughter away from him. He complained about how badly he had been treated. You would have thought he had been an actual presence in Sofia's life, the way he fumed and spouted. I was furious with his selfishness and maniacal behavior.

The attorney didn't know how much it would cost to pursue the adoption process, or if we would even win. It was a daunting expense as we were also planning to buy a home.

I thought of Carlo's and my little bottle of hopes, probably floating somewhere in the Tyrrhenian or Mediterranean. I decided to cast this worry adrift for a while and give it over to the fates that had been kind to us thus far.

We had managed to save money for a substantial down-payment on a home and we began our search. Apartment living with my brother had been fun, but we were ready for some room to move. Carlo and I began exploring neighborhoods, and after a "wrong" turn down a road during our search, we discovered a gated community that appealed to us. Carlo especially liked the feel of the place. It was secluded, bordered by a woodland area with walking trails. We contacted a realtor and asked them to show us some properties in this location.

We looked at five or so houses one day and seemed to have hit our limit. Carlo, not one to miss anything, asked about a house that had a sign in the yard that the realtor hadn't shown us.

"You don't want to see that house," she replied.

"Yes, we do," Carlo countered.

It was a disaster. A casualty of the foreclosure pandemic of the last few years, it had been bank-owned since 2009. It had holes in the walls, stained carpet, a missing drawer in the kitchen, dog hair matted to the baseboards, and a door that had been cut in half! Someone had drawn on the walls and carpet with Sharpies and crayons. Yet, somehow, I could envision raising our family there. I could picture what the house could be, with a little TLC and a LOT of bleach, paint, and "elbow grease". We squared the deal on 3400 square feet of hard work and became homeowners!

Our apartment lease would be up soon, so we rolled up our sleeves and began renovations. Carlo demonstrated his talents in carpentry as he ripped out filthy carpet and cut each new piece of wood flooring himself. My parents came and helped clean and paint. There were many late nights and long weekends, but in time it started to shine like the cozy castle it was meant to be. We moved into our new home in late February of 2014.

And Nora Makes Four

I had suffered more miscarriages since that day back in 2011. It was torture for both Carlo and me. Each time I became pregnant I prayed, held my breath, and considered standing on my head for nine months. We finally resigned ourselves to the possibility that Sofia would be our only child. I looked around me at our beautiful home, my beautiful girl, and my beautiful Carlo. It was enough. Truly. *Enough*.

What is it about yielding to God, or fate, or simple reality that frees up your being? That allows your soul to become fertile ground for more love to be sown and reaped? What is it about the letting go, tossing your dreams into an ocean of chance, all the while accepting the gifts in front of you?

I had taken a temp job at an Orlando hospital that again turned out to be a not-so-temporary position. I was excited for my work: hiring people who helped other people. I knew both sides of that coin, obviously. Not so very long ago I had needed help, and then I became the helper. It was an exciting and fulfilling opportunity.

With my feeling of fulfillment both at home and at work came another fulfillment. Two months into the job, I was pregnant once more. Day by day, week by week, I prayed that this baby would sense the "home" I had found and know that we were ready to receive him or her with all our beings. I sent waves of love into my body and projected a guarded positivism. Quietly, I pleaded with the universe. Weeks became months... we made the announcement at Christmas.

I handed Sofia a card and she read aloud: "You are going to be the best big sister". She looked up at me with her mouth agape. My parents cried. We repeated the "sounding joy" to friends and family at home and abroad: baby Pilia would soon arrive. I needed no other Christmas present.

In the spring, my friends threw a fantastic baby shower for me. Even Baca drove down to join in the festivities! Sofia was over the moon to be a big sister.

"Nora" comes from both Latin and Anglo-Norman origins. It's a popular name in Scotland and Ireland, the diminutive of the classic "Eleanora". It means "honorable". You can visit the ruins of the ancient city of Nora in Sardinia. On August fifth, 2015, our little Nora "honored" us with her presence. My mother and Carlo were there with me while Sofia and Carlo's parents waited outside.

Years before, I had celebrated Sofia's birth with friends and family as I harbored desperation in my mind. I was alone, the one person my daughter had to count on. I was young, naïve, and uncertain. It was not lost on me that my ex and I had chosen the Italian spelling of her name: I believe that was pure prophecy. Sofia means "wise": my little girl had spurred me on to wisdom, bravery, and confidence. I had "honored" her faith in me as her mother and the proof was there in my arms. Little Nora. I looked into Carlo's sparkling eyes and saw us embracing one another amid the green hills over Dublin. When he took Nora in his arms, I pictured him playing with her on the beach at Stintino one day soon. I could breathe and share my little gift with love all around. No fear. No apprehension. Only abundant joy.

#

During my maternity leave I had many visitors, including Aunt Lynn and Pamela. Daniele and Vittoria stayed with us for a few months, helping out while enjoying every second they could with their newest grandchild. My Italian language skills greatly improved during this time.

Upon returning to work, I overheard a colleague discussing her oldest son's stepparent adoption. She commented that the process had been difficult, but that the lawyer was wonderful. Sofia was ten years old. I thought back to my own experience, when my parents had taken me on a picnic at thirteen to tell me about my biological father. It was time to end this gnawing misery of Sofia having a different last name.

Carlo and I contacted the aforementioned attorney and he was relaxed and positive. We had no idea where Sofia's father was living, so the lawyer sent a letter to Jenny's address. I was sitting in my office shortly thereafter and received a phone call from a Dayton number.

My ex raved about how I had stolen his daughter when I moved to Florida and that no judge would agree to the adoption. Though he had not inquired about Sofia one time in ten years, he insisted that I was going to have to start sending Sofia to Ohio to visit him. He hadn't sent one birthday or Christmas present, attended any school function, or even taken her out for lunch since she was six weeks old! I couldn't believe his nerve. In my mind, there I was: driving myself to the hospital as I braved contractions, with my ex sitting beside me, sleepy-eyed and insisting that I stop at Burger King. I shook my head in disgust.

I have not spoken to him since. Our attorney was undaunted and in no time the adoption was granted. Sofia took Carlo's name in January of 2016. The day things were finalized, Carlo and I asked Sofia what she wanted to do to celebrate. Her only request was to go to Michael's craft store and buy rubber bands to make bracelets. We went to Michael's and I think we bought her enough rubber bands, beads, and other assorted accessories to make bracelets for the entire state of Florida.

As for Carlo, he loved Sofia as his own. He had been her father for six years. I think he celebrated the relief that, in the event of anything happening to me, he would be her legal guardian.

My Irish adventure officially concluded that day, with a Sardinian detour and a dream-ending only two hearts like Carlo's and mine could make happen. *Dóthain.* Abbastanza. Enough.

Author's Note

The synchronicity of my life is not lost on me. My mother cut her foot on a piece of glass, which precipitated in her dating and eventually marrying my father. Pamela cut her foot on a piece of glass that evening in Temple Bar, which resulted in our car ride with Carlo and the trip to the chipper. Then, there was my fateful trip with my parents to Emerald Isle, North Carolina, followed by my trip to the original Emerald Isle. Carlo took me to Costa Smeralda, "Emerald Coast", on our first trip to Sardinia. Sofia's birthstone is emerald, while Nora's is peridot.

The emerald is the stone of the heart, symbolizing compassion, mercy, and universal love. I can only hope that I continue to honor life's gems that seem to have been showered upon me by this symbolic talisman.

Green is the color of health, hope, and adventure. I have all these things and more. It is also the color of compassion, which Carlo and I strive to instill in our daughters.

We are happy in our Florida home in between trips to Europe and beyond. My girls are hearty little world-travelers and the light in their grandparents' eyes. I am a professional photographer now, and delight in capturing precious moments for others, as well as my loved ones. Carlo and I still share an incomparable love, grateful every day that my friend Pamela wanted a friend to accompany her to a birthday party in the land of luck.

This book comes from my desire to share my joy and give hope to others. You can make your own luck: you just have to be brave and step out of the box. There are opportunities in front of us, every day. They may seem like nothing. Pay attention. Your life may be hiding behind a friend you have yet to make, a trip you have yet to take, or in a simple gesture like someone offering to drive you home after a long night of libations and revelry. Visualize your dream, keep it in front of you, and you will live it. There is always hope.

*One final note of synchronicity: When I decided to write a book, I phoned my former high school mentor Joyce Case, who had become an author herself, and asked her to recommend an editor. She said that she knew someone through her publishing company and that she would put me in touch. Imagine my amazement when I phoned the woman whom Joyce recommended: she laughed as she told me how "prophetic" my contacting her had been: the woman had spent the first ten years of her childhood in Indiana—in a little hamlet on Highway 3 called…"Sardinia".

Some things are just meant to be.

A Note from Carlo...

"Decisions we make each day lead us where our future will take us..."

These words, from one of Laurie's first emails to me, left an indelible impression. They summarized my general philosophy on life. While growing up in a middle-class, loving family on a small island in Europe, being raised by amazing parents with outstanding moral characters, I knew that there would come a day when I would leave my comfortable cocoon and head out for parts unknown, challenging myself and living life to the fullest.

I remember vividly the day that Laurie showed up in my "garden" in Dublin. I like to say, in a more modern framework, that common acquaintances delivered my wife to me like Amazon Prime. I was impressed with the tall, fit, American blonde with the captivating eyes. I immediately saw something that fascinated me. It was more than enough incentive to accept an invitation to my landlord's daughter's birthday party.

After our brief time together that weekend, I was inspired to make changes in my personal life. I had to email her, to continue our discussion. With every email, I grew more enamored of Laurie and her attitude toward life. I distinctly recall the email in which she told me about Sofia. The fact that a woman with such integrity and positive perspective was raising a child on her own impressed me even more. I immediately shared this fact with my parents and my sister.

Getting to know Laurie was an adventure. The more I got to know her, the more intrigued and fascinated I was. I grew to respect this young woman with the can-do attitude, a woman who had faced adversity head-on and was raising her daughter while holding two and sometimes three jobs. With every email, I grew more certain that this woman had to be my life partner, my wife.

It takes courage to look deep inside yourself, know what you want, and challenge yourself. It would have been easy for me to dismiss my encounter with the beautiful, exuberant American girl as something too far-fetched and geographically inconvenient. It would have been easy not to send that first email. It would have been easy to see the situation as insurmountable: language barriers, cultural differences, not to mention time zones. It would have been easy for Laurie and me to resume our lives after our brief encounter in Ireland. Instead, we chose to face the challenges in our desire to live life "100%". It took planning, hard work, team effort, and sacrifice, but we knew we were destined to create this amazing journey we call "Our Life Together".

This book is a reminder that life is a gift and that settling is not an option. Why limit yourself? Anything is possible if you put your head and heart into it.

Thank you, Laurie, for everything you are.

Carlo

Acknowledgments

Thank you to my beautiful family and friends for all your love and encouragement while writing my story. Your belief in me has allowed me to push through the writing process and see this through to the end. Without writing all your names you know who you are – thank you!

Thank you to my husband, Carlo Pilia, who allowed much of our story to be retold – I am blessed to be married to someone who believes in and loves me so deeply. Thank you to my daughters, Sofia and Nora. I'm so grateful that God sent you to me and allowed me the honor of being your mama.

I am grateful to my mentor and friend, Joyce Case. Thank you for always believing in me and encouraging me to follow my dreams. I am forever thankful for your guidance throughout the entire book writing journey. This would not have been possible without you.

Thank you to my incredible editor Krista Hill of Talbot Editorial Services for believing in and taking on this project. I could not have done this without your dedication and expertise. Thank you for working right alongside me from beginning to end with countless phone calls, emails, updates and edits. I am forever grateful.

Thank you to my dear friend Abigail Augustine Beck for your artistic eye and creative ideas in helping me design the cover for this book. The cover was quite a process and with your help we did it.

Thank you to Beta Books (www.betabooks.co) for your awesome tool for organizing beta reading. As special shout out and thanks for all of my beta readers: Heidi Donovan, Joyce Case, Pamela Allen, Ann Paul, Carina Storrs, Kathy Cosgrave and Carlo Pilia. Your questions, feedback, inquisitive eye and level of detail are invaluable to the completion of my book. You all added your special touch in your own unique way.

Lastly a significant thank you to my parents, Kevin and Susan Henry. I am truly grateful for everything you have done for me. I would not be who I am without your love and support.

We invite you to join Laurie on her socials:

SAY HELLO ANYTIME AT:

Facebook: lauriepiliaauthor
Instagram: lauriepiliaphotography
LinkedIn: Laurie Pilia, PHR, SHRM-CP

Or reach out directly at info@lauriepilia.com
Website: www.lauriepilia.com

Made in United States
Orlando, FL
23 April 2023

32397412R00118